Many people today are recognizing the act that the human person yearns for meaning in life, a meaning which is found in one's relationship with the Creator. Dan Burke's new work on meditation, especially in the thoughts of St. Peter of Alcantara and also reflected in his close collaboration with St. Teresa of Avila, offers significant help in this search. We are made aware that these Saints rejected the notion that meditation is the work of the human mind. Rather, it lies in seeking a quiet and peaceful time with the Living God. Prayer in this work is defined as "A bath, an open place, a bed of pleasure wherein the soul rests and finds refreshment."

Of special interest is Dan Burke's updated translation of St. Peter of Alcantara's treatise on prayer and meditation. This book allows the reader to share in the experience of the Saints who are masters of prayer. This is certainly a growing need to the growing secularism and even implicit atheism which is present in our culture.

—*Most Rev. John J. Myers, Archbishop of Newark*

Dan Burke's presentation of writings of the Franciscan Saint Peter of Alcantara is a welcome addition to the body of Franciscan spirituality. Although initially written some 400 years ago, Saint Peter's approach to a method for meditation, and his practical advice on how to enter into meditation, are of timeless significance and of great value to anyone seeking to foster a deeper Franciscan spirituality. Dan Burke's organization of St. Peter's work prepares the reader to more fully embrace his process for meditation. The reader will feel compelled to return to this book time and time again to grasp the depth of Saint Peter's wisdom and to endeavor to incorporate his teachings into one's daily life.

—*Fr. Sean O. Sheridan, TOR*
President, Franciscan University of Steubenville

St. Teresa of Avila's struggles to describe her mystical experiences to spiritual directors who did not understand led her finally to Peter of Alcantara. She views him as "a very holy and spiritual man" and presents in *The Book of Her Life* a detailed account of his penitential practices with the conclusion that "it seemed he was made of nothing but tree roots." Yet despite all his penances, she found him to be "very affable." She also mentions that he wrote some small books in the vernacular on prayer that are now popular, "for as one who practiced it well himself he wrote in a very helpful way for those who are given to prayer." In her Constitutions she recommends for her nuns, among other books, the books written by Peter of Alcantara. In this English translation by Giles Willoughby we can now, like Teresa, sit at the feet of this master on prayer.

—*Fr. Kieran Kavanaugh, OCD*
Institute of Carmelite Studies and vice postulator
for the canonization of St. Teresa Benedicta of the Cross

In creating this book, it is as if Dan Burke went up into the attic of the Church, brought down a treasure box full of riches, and dusted them off for us all to behold. The wisdom of St. Peter of Alcantara is desperately needed in this day and age, perhaps more than ever before, and many people will be blessed by discovering his insights on the spiritual life.

—*Jennifer Fulwiler*
Author, writer, and atheist convert to Catholicism

The material in this book of meditations is not for the novice, not for the beginner in the Christian life. It is a book of meditations for those who have labored in the vineyard and are willing to be called on to greater holiness. It is a sharp knife that cuts through our self-satisfaction and shows us how much greater and deeper is the love of God, the demands of that Love, which if yielded to, produce the holiness that will truly glorify Him. May He be praised forever in the wisdom of the saints!

—*Sr. Ann Shields, SGL*
Internationally noted conference and retreat speaker,
and author of numerous books on Catholic spirituality

Navigating the Interior Life

Finding God

Through Meditation

Navigating the Interior Life

Interior Life

Finding God

Through Meditation

ST. PETER OF ALCANTARA

Edited by Daniel Burke

EMMAUS
ROAD
PUBLISHING

Steubenville, Ohio
A Division of Catholics United for the Faith
www.emmausroad.org

Emmaus Road Publishing
601 Granard Parkway
Steubenville, Ohio 43952

English edition published as
A Golden Treaty of Mental Prayer, Meditation, and Devotion

Translated by Giles Willoughby 1844
Translation updated and edited by Daniel Burke
Revised edition published © 2015 Daniel Burke
All rights reserved. Published 2015
Printed in the United States of America
19 18 17 16 15 14 1 2 3 4 5 6

Library of Congress Control Number: 2014957461
ISBN: 978-1-63446-016-3

Cover design by Claudia Volkman

Pope Gregory XV for Perpetual Memory of the Event
A true copy taken from volume 3 of Laerzio Cherubini's
Collection of [Papal] Bulls.

Having been appointed by the Lord in See of the Prince of the Apostles, although by no supporting merits of our own, we willingly grant the devout prayers of the faithful, by which the Lord of virtues is glorified in his servants, and we bestow those things with our suitable favor.

Since not only Philip the Third of famous memory, and our son in Christ, the most outstanding Philip the Fourth, Catholic kings of the Spanish people, have been urging it, but also almost all the kingdoms of Spain, and since our reverend brothers, the duly appointed Cardinals of the Holy Roman Church have examined many times by our command the cause of the servant of God, Peter of Alcantara, of the Order of Friars Minor of the stricter observance called Discalced, Founder of the Province of St. Joseph of the same Order, in consequence of a course of testimony of three Auditors of causes of the Apostolic Palace for the accomplishment of the canonization; and furthermore because of many sessions held at the recommendation of our beloved son Marco Antonio, priest of the titular church of St. Eusebius, Cardinal Gonzadino, [the cardinals] have pronounced that [the cause] is completely firm in the validity of proceedings, in the fame of his holiness, faith, purity, in the rest of his virtues not only in general but also in particular, and in the veneration of his relics and of his tomb, and finally very many miracles; and they have decreed that We are able to declare whenever we wish, according to the rite of the Catholic Church, that the same servant of God is a Saint and reigning in heaven, and that We are able to propose by solemn canonization that he is worthy of veneration by all the faithful.

But as the aforesaid King Philip the Fourth, and the Minister General of our beloved son, and the aforesaid Brothers of the order have made humble supplication to us, we deign to grant by Apostolic kindness that until the canonization of the aforesaid Peter should occur, the same Peter may be called Blessed Peter and that for him a Mass may be celebrated and, as below, the office to be recited for him as a for a Confessor who is not a Pope in his honor. We, having been moved by their supplications of this kind, [grant] that a Mass and office may be celebrated and recited for him as for a Confessor who is not a Pope, on the 19th day of October, on which the memory of his death will be celebrated everywhere on earth by the whole Order of the Observant Minors of both sexes.

But in the town of Alcantara, belonging to no diocese, where he was born, and in the other town from the Arenas of the Diocese of Avila where we have heard that his body is resting, it is entirely permissible for both regular and secular clerics to celebrate it with a semi-duplex rite.

And finally we grant and allow by Apostolic authority by the course of present things forever in the aforesaid Province of St. Joseph, of which he was the founder, that the Office and the Mass according to the rubrics of the Breviary and the Roman Missal, are able to be celebrated with an octave just as for a Patron.

The constitutions and Apostolic ordinances, and whatever contrary things notwithstanding.

We wish however that the trust of those things present also be immediately shown everywhere to these things written below, having been adopted and also impressed by the hand of a certain Notary Public, and secured by the seal of the person constituted in Ecclesiastical authority, which would be granted to them if they were exhibited or shown to the present things.

Given at Rome in St. Peter's under the ring of the Fisherman, on April 18th, 1622, in the second year of our Pontificate.

TABLE OF CONTENTS

INTRODUCTION

St. Teresa of Avila and St. Peter of Alcantara—Controversy and Insight

In 1577, St. Teresa of Avila completed what is heralded as her seminal work on prayer, the *Interior Castle*. This guidebook to the most profound depths of prayer has become the standard against which all serious inquiries into interior progress must be measured. This is the reason that it is to St. Teresa that the Catechism of the Catholic Church poses the question, "What is contemplative prayer?"

It is in the fourth mansion of the *Interior Castle* that the author of this work, the holy Franciscan Friar, Peter of Alcantara, through his writings and relationship with St. Teresa, collaborates with her in an important exchange that should impact the way we view prayer today.

This collaboration arose from a dispute involving individuals positing to St. Teresa that a soul seeking to advance in prayer should work to manage thoughts or guide the mind to silence or stillness during prayer. Those advancing this idea cited St. Peter's writings as proof of the veracity of their claims.

Owing to her knowledge of and respect for St. Peter, as he was one of her spiritual directors, St. Teresa desired to ensure that her thinking on the matter was correct. She turned to the text you now hold to resolve the dispute.

After her investigation, St. Teresa, not known for timidity of expression and emboldened by her union with St. Peter, attacked these false teachings with a notable force that should elicit our careful attention.

St. Teresa, in the third chapter of the fourth mansion of the *Interior Castle* argued four key points against using any method that is excessively focused on thought management during prayer. In summary, she argues that recollection is a loving awareness of the Lord that comes in the form of a gift and not as a result of spiritual gymnastics. Teresa argues that, as we become absorbed in the Lord, it is insufficient, stifling, frustrating and even dangerous to strive for some inert state of consciousness in which we act against our desire to understand. Instead of a state of consciousness, she encourages us to seek a loving friendship with God:

1) Deeper prayer does not require that we manage our thoughts (which she calls "human industry") but that we seek to simply and humbly yield to the work of the Lord. Otherwise, she argues, the result will be that we further exacerbate the normal challenges of prayer.

2) Deeper prayer comes through a resignation to the will to God. This resignation brings peace, whereas human efforts bring frustration. Psychologically coercing ourselves to inactivity disturbs the true peace that the Lord wants to grant. Peace is a matter of bringing our created will into harmony with the loving Will that created it. Teresa, who understands the delicacy of spousal friendship with the Lord, is aware that on this point true peace requires a completely free response of the heart to the Lord's self-disclosure. When we do not give space to the heart to make such a free response through petitionary prayer and meditation, we are trying to surmount the movements God Himself has inspired in it. Such coercion always does more harm than good.

3) "Because the same care which is employed for thinking on nothing, will, perhaps, excite the imagination to think much" instead. The effort to achieve a state of thoughtlessness can exacerbate the soul into thinking in even more distracting ways than otherwise would have been the case. We become aware that we are thinking not to think or else that we have achieved a state of thoughtlessness. But this awareness of our own mental activity or inertia, whether self-congratulatory or condemning, attends not to God or what He discloses but to self. It is locked in an orbit around one's own big fat ego, unable to break free of its self-awareness even when it is not self-aware.

4) "Because the most pleasing and substantial service we can do for God is to have only His honor and glory in view, and to forget ourselves, our own benefit, delight, and pleasure." Pursuing a psychic state can be a preoccupation and distraction when our attention should be on the Lord and on responding to His Presence. This is the same problem addressed in Teresa's third point, but presented from the perspective of our friendship with God, the perspective out of which she begins her critique. If we are self-occupied with self-awareness or lack of self-awareness, thinking or not thinking, understanding or not understanding, we have already lost sight of the Lord. Our prayer is not a response of love to the One who loves us. Rather than the devotion of friendship and awareness of the otherness of God, rather than being vulnerable to adoration before the wonder of the Lord, we have fixated on things that will never expand the heart or allow it to be humble before Him.

Teresa continues her argument with the admonition that we should not seek to "charm our faculties" into some false state of readiness for God, but that if our mind or faculties are ever to be suspended or managed, then the valid impetus or force to achieve such an end comes from

God alone. We need do nothing but simply turn our attention to Him and occupy our minds with Him in prayer, which is the central thrust of this book and of the practice of authentic Christian meditation.

Why was this so important to Teresa then, and why is it important to us now? We live in a period that is just as obsessed with methods of prayer and false teaching on prayer as it was then. In keeping with our lower nature, we look for secret, easy formulas to success; five ways to a better this, and four quick and easy ways to a better that. As with modern weight loss schemes, these methods leave the wallet thinner and the soul no closer to the fulfillment of what it truly needs and desires. St. Peter of Alcantara's work is as sure an antidote to much of the false teaching of our day as it was in his own.

An Overview

St. Peter's insights on prayer are far more profound and far reaching than the size of this text might suggest. The reader will find not only help in satisfying the short-term need for insight on how to grow in prayer, but also a window into perspectives on prayer that should challenge and enrich the reader for years to come.

In particular, St. Peter is not afraid to call us to a deeper commitment to self-denial and ascetical practices as we pursue a deeper life of prayer and devotion. Many in our time criticize or downplay traditional asceticism, but if we believe St. Teresa's account of St. Peter's appearance to her after his death, it seems that God also approved of his approach. We also have affirmation of his ascetical counsels affirmed and even more deeply explored in the writings of St. John of the Cross.

St. Peter's Understanding of Progress in Prayer

One of the greatest benefits of our time with respect to theological clarity is St. John Paul II's gift of the Catechism of the Catholic Church. In part four entitled *Christian Prayer*, we have a beautiful and concise summary of all of the most important aspects of the Church's understanding of prayer. Here, in the Catechism, we see distinctions made between three expressions of prayer: vocal prayer, meditation, and contemplation. This clarity allows us to better understand the progressive nature of the development of prayer and corrects a number of past and present errors. It also sheds light on and reinforces St. Peter's use of the terms "meditation" and "contemplation."

St. Peter's use of the term "meditation" falls squarely in line with the Catechism wherein it reveals:

2705 Meditation is above all a quest. The mind seeks to understand the why and how of the Christian life, in order to adhere and respond to what the Lord is asking. The required attentiveness is difficult to sustain. We are usually helped by books, and Christians do not want for them: the Sacred Scriptures, particularly the Gospels, holy icons, liturgical texts of the day or season, writings of the spiritual fathers, works of spirituality, the great book of creation, and that of history—the page on which the "today" of God is written.

2706 To meditate on what we read helps us to make it our own by confronting it with ourselves. Here, another book is opened: the book of life. We pass from thoughts to reality. To the extent that we are humble and faithful, we discover in meditation the movements that stir the heart and we are able to discern them. It is a question of acting truthfully in order to come into the light: "Lord, what do you want me to do?"

2707 There are as many and varied methods of meditation as there are spiritual masters. Christians owe it to themselves to develop the desire to meditate regularly, lest they come to resemble the three first kinds of soil in the parable of the sower. But a method is only a guide; the important thing is to advance, with the Holy Spirit, along the one way of prayer: Christ Jesus.

2708 Meditation engages thought, imagination, emotion, and desire. This mobilization of faculties is necessary in order to deepen our convictions of faith, prompt the conversion of our heart, and strengthen our will to follow Christ. Christian prayer tries above all to meditate on the mysteries of Christ, as in *lectio divina* or the Rosary. This form of prayerful reflection is of great value, but Christian prayer should go further: to the knowledge of the love of the Lord Jesus, to union with him.

St. Peter also clearly acknowledges meditation as a transitional form of prayer (as do all faithful spiritual theologians) that draws us ever more deeply into relationship with God. With God's grace, we eventually transition *out* of this mode of prayer, into a more simple prayer, and then to what is known as infused contemplation. St. Peter clarifies this process. In his discussion of contemplation, he uses the term "contemplation" to refer to either acquired/natural contemplation or affective meditation. However, he is particularly clear on this matter in his eighth counsel on meditation, where he reveals the right understanding of a kind of contemplation that is much different than what can be known in meditation and is in keeping with St. Teresa's understanding of contemplation.

The importance of this clarity is a matter of significance in our time. As Ignatian spirituality has emerged as a dominant expression today, a particular form of Ignatian meditation has become very popular. This approach to prayer has and will continue to bear much fruit in the lives of those who diligently engage with the practice, especially in the manner proposed by St. Peter. It is a form of prayer that is important to help beginners emerge through and then out of the purgative phase of spiritual growth into the illuminative phase. This transition, most clearly revealed in the writings of St. John of the Cross, is one whereby the pilgrim, once deeply blessed by meditation, leaves it behind in favor of a contemplation wherein God rewards their diligent ascesis and devotion by drawing them into a form of prayer that has little to do with human will or action and much more to do with God's work of transformative grace in the soul.

Much more can be said about the value of this great gift of meditation to the Church. This text is so clear that the reader should have little trouble finding the gems that God has in store for all who truly desire to grow in relationship with Him in prayer.

Sanctity as the Source of Wisdom in St. Peter of Alcantara

Much can be gained through an exploration of Friar Peter's sanctity, found in the unedited treatment of his life which we placed in the appendix. It is notable to us that there are few that St. Teresa praised as heartily as St. Peter. One prime example is found in chapter twenty-seven of her autobiography:

And what an excellent likeness in the person of that blessed friar, Peter of Alcantara, God has just taken from us! The world cannot bear such perfection now; it is said that men's health is grown feebler, and that we are not now in those former times. But this holy man lived in our day; he had a spirit strong as those of another age, and so he trampled on the world. If men do not go about barefooted, nor undergo sharp penances, as he did, there are many ways, as I have said before,[1] of trampling on the world; and our Lord teaches them when He finds the necessary courage. How great was the courage with which His Majesty filled the Saint I am speaking of! He did penance—oh, how sharp it was!—for seven-and-forty years, as all men know. I should like to speak of it, for I know it to be all true.

He spoke of it to me and to another person, from whom he kept few or no secrets. As for me, it was the affection he bore me that led him to speak; for it was our Lord's will that he should undertake my defense, and encourage me, at a time when I was in great straits, as I said before, and shall speak of again. He told me, I think, that for forty years he slept but an hour and a half out of the twenty-four, and that the most laborious penance he under-

---

1. Teresa of Ávila, *The Life of St. Teresa of Jesus of the Order of Our Lady of Carmel*, trans. David Lewis (LaVergne, TN: Bottom of the Hill Publishing, 2010), ch. 14, sec. 7.

went, when he began, was this of overcoming sleep. For that purpose, he was always either kneeling or standing. When he slept he sat down, his head resting against a piece of wood driven into the wall. Lie down he could not, if he wished it; for his cell, as everyone knows, was only four feet and a half in length. In all these years, he never covered his head with his hood, even when the sun was hottest, or the rain heaviest. He never covered his feet: the only garment he wore was made of sackcloth, and that was as tight as it could be, with nothing between it and his flesh; over this, he wore a cloak of the same stuff. He told me that, in the severe cold, he used to take off his cloak, and open the door and the window of his cell, in order that when he put his cloak on again, after shutting the door and the window, he might give some satisfaction to his body in the pleasure it might have in the increased warmth. His ordinary practice was to eat but once in three days. He said to me, "Why are you astonished at it? It is very possible for anyone who is used to it." One of his companions told me that he would be occasionally eight days without eating: that must have been when he was in prayer; for he was subject to trances, and to the impetuosities of the love of God, of which I was once a witness myself.

His poverty was extreme; and his mortification, from his youth, was such,—so he told me,—that he was three years in one of the houses of his Order without knowing how to distinguish one friar from another, otherwise than by his voice; for he never raised his eyes: and so, when he was obliged to go from one part of the house to the other, he never knew the way, unless he followed the friars. His journeys, also, were made in the same way. For many years, he never saw a woman's face. He told me that it was nothing to him then whether he saw it or not: but he was an aged man when I made his acquaintance; and his weakness was so great, that he seemed like nothing else but the roots of trees. With all his sanctity, he was very agreeable; though his words were few, unless when he was asked questions, he was very pleasant to speak to, for he had a most clear understanding.

Many other things I should like to say of him, if I were not afraid, my father, that you will say, Why does she meddle here? and it is in that fear I have written this. So I leave the subject, only saying that his last end was like his life—preaching to, and exhorting, his brethren. When he saw that the end was come, he repeated the Psalm, "I rejoiced in these things which were said to me"; and then, kneeling down, he died.

Since then, it has pleased our Lord that I should find more help from him than during his life. He advises me in many matters. I have often seen him in great glory. The first time he appeared to me, he said: "O blessed penance, which has merited so great a reward!" with other things. A year before his death he appeared to me, being then far away. I knew he was about to die, and so I sent him word to that effect, when he was some leagues from here. When he died, he appeared to me, and said that he was going to his rest. I did not believe it. I spoke of it to some persons, and within eight days came the news that he was dead—or, to speak more correctly, he had begun to live for evermore.

Behold here, then, how that life of sharp penance is perfected in such glory: and now he is a greater comfort to me, I do believe, than he was on earth. Our Lord said to me on one occasion, that persons could not ask Him anything in his name, and He not hear them. I have recommended many things to him that he was to ask of our Lord, and I have seen my petitions granted. God be blessed for ever! Amen.[2]

Finally, readers familiar with other publications of this work will notice significant differences in this edition. First, we have not included the text commonly attached to this work, as it has been discovered to be written by someone other than St. Peter. In addition, many have found the approach confusing, in seeming to contradict St. Peter's work in both tone and substance. Second, his original ordering of the book provides the meditations themselves prior to the treatment on *how* to meditate. To aid the reader, we simply reversed this order and included more helpful section titles. The final change we made was to update this fine translation to something closer to modern English. We attempted

---

2. Teresa of Ávila, *The Life of St. Teresa of Jesus*, ed. Benedict Zimmerman, trans. David Lewis, fifth ed., (London: Thomas Baker, 1916), 242–45.

to leave all but the most distracting elements of style and period expression in order to allow for the appropriate flavor of a text from a different time to remain intact. We hope to draw the reader out of an everyday casual reading experience up to a higher, or more challenging, deliberate order of reflection which will more likely yield new perspectives on prayer that might otherwise be missed in a text of more common expression. In all of these slight changes, we have sought to diligently remain true to his original thought.

And so it is that we have this great treatise on meditation from St. Peter which with great perfection fulfills St. Teresa's admonition that we have "only His honor and glory in view." Let us focus all of our attention on Him and allow Him to do with us as He wills.

Dan Burke

PERSPECTIVE ON MEDITATION AND DEVOTION

In this chapter we will briefly set down the fruit of prayer and meditation, that men considering the benefit of them may be incited with a prompt and more willing mind to frequent these holy exercises. It is most certain that the malice of our own heart is the principal cause that hinders us from attaining to our beatitude and everlasting happiness, because it makes us slow to godly actions, dull to virtuous exercises, and suggests a greater difficulty in them than there is, which if it were not, a man might walk without any trouble in the way of virtue, and at length without labor attain to his desired end. Hence, it is, that the Apostle says: "I am delighted with the law of God according to the inward man, but I see another law in my members fighting against the law of my mind, and captivating me in the law of sin" (Rom 7:22–23).

The Efficacy of Devotion

This, therefore, is the prime root and cause of our miseries, against which there is no remedy more convenient and efficacious than devotion, which, according to St. Thomas, is nothing else but a certain promptitude and facility of the mind to do well. It excludes from our mind this tedious difficulty and makes us with alacrity apply ourselves to virtuous acts. Therefore, not without cause we may term it spiritual food, recreative and heavenly dew, a pleasant instinct and supernatural affection of the Holy Spirit which so strengthens and transforms the hearts of men that it births in them a new energy and feeling of spiritual things and, on the contrary, a tedious loathing of worldly vanities.

Daily experience manifests this particular reality to us. For we see the souls of those who arise from profound and devout prayer to be strengthened with admirable resolutions, adorned with new graces, and replenished with firm purposes of amendment of life, and frequenting pious exercises, they burn with an ardent desire of serving and loving him with their whole heart, whom in their prayer have found the God of all goodness and kindness, desiring to suffer any grievous and burdensome cross whatsoever it be, yea to shed their blood for his sake. To conclude, prayer is a bath, an open place, a bed of pleasure wherein the soul rests and finds refreshment in God.

By What Means Devotion is Acquired

If you ask me what be the chiefest means to attain unto this heroical virtue of devotion, I answer with the same Doctor, that it is by serious meditation and contemplation of heavenly things. For the ruminating of these in the soul, with a more attentive and profound consideration, births in the will that disposition which we call devotion, which effectually inspires and encourages a man forward to every good work. For this cause, the exercise of prayer and meditation was frequent and familiar to men of sanctity, as judging it the easiest means to develop devotion, which, although it be but one simple virtue, yet it disposes and makes us fit for all others and, as it were, with spurs to a horse, prods us forward to the performance of every good work.

I call St. Bonaventure to witness what I say: His words are these:

The inestimable virtue of prayer is able to obtain all good, and remove all hurtful things. If thou wilt patiently endure adversity, be a man of prayer. If thou wilt overcome tribulation and temptations, be a man of prayer. If thou wilt trample upon thy perverse inclinations, be a man of prayer. If thou wilt know the deceits of Satan, and avoid them, be a man of prayer. If thou wilt live joyfully in the work of God, and trace the way of labor and affliction, be a man of prayer. If thou wilt exercise thyself in a spiritual course, and not walk according to the desires of the flesh, be a man of prayer. If thou wilt put to flight thy vain and trifling fancies, be a man of prayer. If thou wilt feast thy soul with holy thoughts, good desires, fervour, and devotion, be a man of prayer. If thou wilt establish thy heart with a manly spirit, and constant purpose in the service of God, be a man of prayer. To conclude, if thou wilt root out vice, and be endued with virtues, be a man of prayer. In it is received the unction of the Holy Ghost, which teacheth all things. Also, if thou wilt climb up to the top of contemplation, and enjoy the sweet embracings of thy beloved spouse, be a man of prayer. For by the exercise of prayer, we come to that contemplation and taste of heavenly things. Thou seest of what great power and virtue prayer is. For the confirmation of all which, omitting the testimony of holy Scriptures, let this be an evident proof unto thee, that by daily experience, we hear and see illiterate and simple persons to have attained the aforesaid and greater things by the virtue of prayer.[1]

Thus St. Bonaventure.

I beseech you, can there be found a richer treasure or a more fertile field desired? Hear another Doctor no less for religion and sanctity, who upon the same matter says:

By prayer the soul is cleansed from sin, replenished with charity, confirmed in faith, strengthened, and refreshed in spirit. Prayer establisheth the inward man, pacifieth the heart, knoweth the truth, conquereth temptations, expelleth sorrow, reneweth the senses, stirreth up languishing virtue, putteth to flight tepidity, and scoureth the rust of vices. In prayer, the quick sparkles of celestial desires are incessantly sent forth, from the burning coals

---

1. *Meditations of the Life of Christ*, ch. 73, is a work discovered to be written by Joannes a Caulibus rather than St. Bonaventure.

of divine love. The privileges of prayer are rare, the prerogatives admirable. Prayer unlocketh the gates of heaven, manifesteth divine secrets, and always findeth free access to the ears of God.

I will add no more, for those things which have already been said abundantly express the fruits of this holy exercise.

Of Six Things Necessary to Prayer

These are the exercises and meditations, Christian reader, wherewith every day you may feed your soul, which if you do rightly use, you will never want matter to engage your mind devoutly. But note that meditation, if it be well performed, ought to consist of six parts; some of which go before, others follow mental prayer.

Preparation: First, before we apply ourselves to meditation, it is necessary that our mind and soul be diligently prepared for this holy exercise; as the strings of an instrument, except they be beforehand well-tuned, will never make a pleasant melody.

Reading: After preparation ought to follow the reading of some holy mystery, according to the distribution of days in the week, which in beginners is chiefly necessary, until with continual use and custom, matter of meditation offers itself unto their memories.

Meditation: [After reading follows meditation, which is sometimes of such things as can be represented to our imagination: as the life and Passion of our Blessed Savior; the final judgment; hell; and the kingdom of heaven.]

Giving Thanks: [After meditation follows giving of thanks, the occasion of which must be taken from the matter meditated upon.]

Oblation: Then insist upon the matter to be meditated upon. To meditation we must join devout and sincere giving of thanks to God for all his benefits; then a general oblation of all the life of Christ for recompense of any benefit, and our own works to the honor and glory of God.

Petition: Last of all, petition, which is chiefly called prayer, wherein we desire all things necessary for our own salvation, of our neighbors and the good of the whole Church.

These six parts are required to mental prayer, which besides other commodities, minister abundant matter for meditation, seeing they set before us diverse sorts of meats, that if one will not relish our spiritual taste, we may fall upon another; if we be deficient in one, in another we may employ our minds, and kindle our devotion. But in every meditation, neither all these parts nor order is always necessary, although, as I said before, to young beginners it is, that they should have a certain method, according to which they are to guide themselves; wherefore, in that which has or shall be said, my intention is not to set down a hard rule, or immutable perpetual laws, the violating of which should be a fault; but my meaning is to introduce, and bring young beginners and novices into the right way and method of meditation; which, when they are once in use, experience, but especially the Holy Spirit, will better inform them.

Of the Preparation Necessary to Prayer

It will not be beside our purpose to handle all these parts severally; we will, therefore, first begin with preparation, which we did put first. He, therefore, who goes about to meditate, after he has placed his body after a decent manner either kneeling or standing, or composing himself in manner of a cross, or prostrating himself upon the ground, or sitting, if infirmity or necessity does so require, let him first sign himself with the Sign of the Cross; then let him recollect the dispersed powers of his soul, especially the imagination, and sequester it from all temporal and transitory things. Let him elevate his understanding to God, considering his divine presence, with what due reverence and attention is requisite; and let him imagine Almighty God himself to be present in his soul, as in reality he is. If it be the morning meditation, after a general act of contrition for his sins, let him make to God a general confession; if in the evening, let him examine his conscience concerning all his thoughts, words and works of that day; of the forgetfulness of the benefits of Almighty God; and of the sins of his former life; humbly prostrating himself in the sight of the Divine Majesty, in whose presence he now is, after a particular manner, saying the words of the patriarch Abraham: "I will speak to my Lord, seeing I am but dust and ashes" (Gen 18:27). And singing the psalm: "To thee have I lifted up my eyes, who dwellest in the heavens. Behold, as the eyes of servants are on the hands of their masters; as the eyes of the handmaid are on the hands of her mistress: so are our eyes unto our Lord God, until he have mercy on us. Have mercy on us, O Lord, have mercy on us." (Ps 122).

And because we are not able of ourselves to think any good, but all our sufficiency is from God; and because none can say Lord Jesus, that is to say, call upon the name of Jesus, without the Holy Spirit (1 Cor 12:3), to thee, therefore, O Holy Ghost, do I turn myself, with tears imploring thy assistance: "Come, Holy Ghost, send forth from heaven the glittering beams of true light; come, father of the poor; come, giver of rewards; come, light of our hearts, sweet comforter, sweet guest of the soul, sweet refreshing, rest in labor, temperature in heat, in mourning a grateful solace, O blessed light, replenish the hearts of the faithful." Then follows the prayer, "God, who [did instruct] the hearts of the faithful . . . [by the light of the Holy Spirit]," etc. These being said, he shall pray to God to bestow upon him his divine grace, to assist at this holy exercise, with that attention, due recollection, fear and reverence fitting to so great a majesty, humbly beseeching him, so to pass over this time of holy prayer that he may return from thence fortified with new fervor, to execute whatsoever shall belong to his holy service; for prayer which bears not this fruit is lukewarm, imperfect, and of no value before God.

The Way of Meditation

Of Reading

After a due preparation follows reading those things that are to be meditated upon; that must not be too hasty, but mature, serious and quiet; to which the understanding must not only be attentive, to understand those things which are read, but also, and chiefly, the will; that those things which are understood may give a spiritual gust and feeling. When the reader falls upon any place which much moves his affection, let him there pause awhile, that in his heart it may cause a greater impression. He must also beware not to spend too much time in reading, thereby to hinder meditation, it being a more fruitful exercise; for as much as things attentively considered pierce more inwardly and produce greater effect.

What to do when the mind is distracted: If, peradventure, sometime it happens that the mind be so dispersed that it cannot settle itself to prayer, then it is better to insist awhile longer in reading, or to join reading to meditation; or alter the reading of one point, to pause upon that awhile, then after the same manner to proceed to the others: although the understanding tied to certain words which are read cannot so freely be carried into diverse affections, as when it is free from this bond.

In putting out of unprofitable thoughts, great effort is to be used: It is oftentimes very profitable for a man to strive to expel his distracting thoughts; after the example of the patriarch Jacob, manfully to wrestle against them, persevering unto the end: after which fight, the victory being obtained, God does, for the most part, give greater devotion, or more pure contemplation or some other supernatural gift, which he never denies to those who faithfully fight in his cause.

Of Meditation

After reading follows meditation, which is sometimes of such things as can be represented to our imagination: as the life and Passion of our Blessed Savior; the final judgment; hell; and the kingdom of heaven. Sometimes of such things as are subject rather to the understanding than imagination: as the consideration of Almighty God's benefits, his bounty, clemency and other perfections which are in God. These meditations are called, the one intellectual, the other imaginary. Both of which, in these exercises, are to be used after a different manner, as occasion requires. When the meditation is imaginary, so that the thing meditated upon has never had any actual existence or being (in an exact sense), we must so frame and represent it to our imagination, as though we were present in the same place and saw with our eyes those things which were there done. This representation will make the consideration of these things more vivacious and cause a greater impression in our souls; for if our imagination can comprehend whole cities and countries, with less difficulty can it comprehend one mystery. This helps much to the recollection of the mind; this will retain the same busied in itself as a bee in a hive, where she works and disposes all things diligently. But in these things a moderation must be used; for to run with an overly active imagination to Jerusalem, to frame to the imagination those things which are to be meditated there, does oftentimes hurt the head. Wherefore, it is good to abstain from immoderate imaginations, lest nature, oppressed with too violent apprehensions, becomes infirm and weak.

Of Giving Thanks

After meditation follows giving of thanks, the occasion of which must be taken from the matter meditated upon. For example, if the meditation be of the Passion of our Savior, we must give thanks unto him, that he has redeemed us from so great torments. If of sins, that with forbearance he has expected us to do penance. If of the miseries of this life, that he has preserved us from the greatest part of them. If of death, that hitherto, he has defended us from the perils of sudden death and has favorably granted us time of penance. If of the glory of paradise, that he has created us to that end; that after the storms and troubles of this present life, we should enjoy eternal felicity; after this manner, we are to proceed in other meditations. To these benefits, we may join the others which we handled before, to wit, the benefits of our creation, conservation, redemption, and vocation.

As much as in us lies, let us give him thanks: that he has created us after his own image and likeness; that he has given us a memory to remember him; an understanding to know him, and a will to love him; that he has committed us to the custody of angels; that by the help of our angel guardian he has exempted us from many dangers, preserved us from many mortal sins, defended us from death and malice of the devil, while we were in this case, (which was no less than to free us from everlasting death, to which, by sin, we were obnoxious.) That he would vouchsafe to assume our nature upon him and for our sakes suffer a most ignominious death; that we were born of Christian parents; that we were regenerated by Baptism; that in this present life, he has promised grace and unspeakable glory in the world to come; that he has adopted us for his sons; that in the Sacrament of Confirmation, he has fortified us with strong weapons to fight against the world, the flesh and the devil; that he has given himself to us in the Sacrament of the altar; that he has left unto us the Sacrament of Penance, to recover the grace which was lost by mortal sin; that he has visited us daily with good and holy inspirations; that he has given us grace to persevere in holy and pious exercises. After the same method, we must proceed in accounting other of Almighty God's benefits, as well general as particular, and for all, public or private, manifest or secret, give him thanks; and we must invite all creatures, celestial and terrestrial, to bear us company in this holy exercise, singing the song of the three children: "All ye works of the Lord, bless the Lord: praise and exalt him above all for ever" (Dan 3:57). And the psalm, "Bless the Lord, O my soul: and let all that is within me bless his holy name. Bless the Lord, O my soul, and never forget all that he hath done for thee. Who forgiveth all thy iniquities; who healeth all thy diseases. Who redeemeth thy life from destruction, who crowneth thee with mercy and compassion" (Ps 102:1–4).

Of Oblation

Cordial thanks being given to God, presently the heart breaks naturally into that affection, which the kingly prophet David felt in himself, when he said: "What shall I render to our Lord, for all things that he hath rendered to me?" (Ps 115:12). Which desire, we shall in some sort satisfy, if we offer to God whatsoever we have. First, therefore, we must offer to God ourselves, for his perpetual servants, wholly resigning ourselves to his holy will, howsoever he shall please to dispose of us. We must likewise direct all our thoughts, words, and works, whatsoever we shall do or suffer, to the supreme honor and glory of his sacred name. Then we must offer to God the Father all the merits of his only begotten Son, all the labors and sorrows he did undergo, in this miserable world, to fulfill the will of his heavenly Father, beginning from his nativity and hard manger, to his contemptuous crucifying and giving up his spirit; forasmuch as these are all the goods and means whereof in the New Testament he has left us heirs; wherefore, as that is no less our own, which is given us freely, than that we get with our industry; so the merits of Christ, which he freely bestowed upon us, are no less our own than if we attained them with our sweat and labor. Hence every man may offer this sacred oblation as the first, numbering one by one, all the labors and virtues of the life of Christ, his obedience, patience, humility, charity and his other virtues, seeing these are the most excellent of all oblations that we can offer to God.

Of Petition

This noble oblation being well performed, we may securely and confidently proceed to the asking of any gifts and graces. First, therefore, Almighty God is to be prayed to with inflamed charity and ardent zeal of his divine honor, for the conversion of all nations, that all people may be illuminated with the knowledge of him, praying and adoring him as the only true and living God. To this end, from the bottom of our hearts, we may utter the words of the kingly prophet: "Let people, O God, confess to thee ; let all people give praise to thee" (Ps 66:4). Then, we must pray to God for the prelates of the Church, the supreme pastor, cardinals, archbishops, bishops, and other prelates, that he would be pleased so to govern and illuminate them, with the light of his heavenly grace, that they may be able to bring all men to the knowledge and obedience of their Creator. We must also pray to God for kings and princes, (as St. Paul admonishes) and for all men placed in authority, that by their diligent care, their subjects may live a quiet life, well instructed with honest manners, for this is grateful to God, that wills all should be saved and come to the knowledge of his truth. Then for all the members of his Mystical Body; for the just, that he would be pleased to conserve them in their sanctity; for sinners, to convert them from their wicked courses to the amendment of their lives; for the dead, that he would free them from the expiating torments wherein they are detained and bring them to their eternal rest.

We must pray to God for the poor infirm captives, bond-slaves, or others, in whatsoever tribulation; that for the merits of his dear Son, he would vouchsafe to help and free them from all their miseries. After we have prayed for the good of our neighbors, let us, at length, intreat for our own necessities, which discretion will teach everyone in particular (if he be not altogether ignorant of himself) what they are. But, that we may set down a method for beginners, we will lead them into this pathway.

First, therefore we must pray to God, that through the merits and Passion of his only begotten Son, he would pardon our sins, give us grace to avoid them and to expiate them with good works worthy of penance; but especially, to implore for help and assistance against those evil inclinations and vices in which we are most addicted, laying open to our heavenly physician all the wounds of our diseased souls, that with the ointment of holy grace he would heal them.

Then, let us ask for the most excellent virtues wherein the whole perfection of a Christian man consists; for example, faith, hope, charity, fear, humility, patience, obedience, fortitude in adversity, poverty of spirit, contempt of the world, true discretion, purity of intention, and others like to these, which are placed in the supreme top of a spiritual building.

- Faith is the prime root and foundation of a Christian.
- Hope is a staff to defend us from all tribulations of this present life.
- Charity is the end of all perfection.
- Fear of God is the beginning of true wisdom.
- Humility is the basis and ground work of all virtues.
- Patience is the strongest armour against the fury of our enemies.
- Obedience is the most grateful oblation to God, wherein man offers himself for a sacrifice.
- Discretion is the eye of the soul.
- Fortitude the hand thereof, wherewith it brings all works unto perfection.
- Purity of intention directs all her actions unto God.

We must after pray for other virtues which may help us forward in the way of perfection; as moderation in meat and drink, moderation of the tongue, custody of the senses, modesty and composition of the outward man, sweetness in giving good example to our neighbours, rigor and severity towards ourselves, and the like.

Last of all, we must conclude this petition with a fervent imploring of the divine love and here to pause awhile, so that the chiefest part of time be spent in an earnest desiring of this grace and favor, seeing in the divine love all our joy consists of, to that end, this prayer following will not be unprofitable.

A Prayer for Obtaining Divine Love

Grant, I beseech you, O Lord, that I may love you with all my soul, with all my heart, with all my strength; O my only hope, my perfect glory, my refuge and solace; O my dearest of all friends, sweet spouse, flourishing spouse, sweeter than any honey, delight of my heart, life of my soul, joy of my spirit; O bright day of eternity, clear light of my bowels, paradise of my heart, original of all my good; O my chiefest strength, prepare, O Lord in my soul a delicious resting place, that according to your promise, there you may dwell and make your mansion. Mortify in me whatsoever is displeasing to you, and make me a man according to your own heart. Pierce the marrow of my soul, wound my heart with the darts of dear affection, and inebriate me with the wine of love. When shall I perfectly please you in all things? When shall I cast from me all things contrary to you? When shall I be wholly yours? When shall I leave to be my own? When shall nothing live in me but what is yours? When shall I embrace you with ardent affection? When will you inflame and consume me with the flames of love? When will you pierce and replenish me on every side with your sweetness? When will you lay open and manifest to my poverty that precious kingdom which is within me, that is to say, your sacred self, with all your riches? When will you unite me perfectly unto you? When will you transform and swallow me up wholly in you, that from you I may never depart? When will you remove from me all obstacles, which hinder me, that are not one spirit with you?

O beloved of my soul! O delight of my heart, look down upon me and hear me, not for my own merits, but out of your infinite goodness instruct, illuminate, direct, and help me in all and through all, that I neither speak or do anything but that which I shall know to be grateful before your sight. O my God, my love, my joy, my pleasure, my fortress, and my life! Why do you not help the poor and needy imploring your assistance? You who fill heaven and earth, why do you suffer my heart to be empty? You who cloathe the flowers and lilies of the fields with beauty; you who nourish the birds of the air; you who sustain the least creature of the earth; why are you unmindful of me, that forgets all things for the love of you? O immense goodness! I had knowledge of you too late, that I loved you no sooner. O new and ancient beauty! O miserable was my state, when I lived without your love! O wretched was my condition, when I knew you not! Intolerable blindness of my heart, when I saw you not! I sought you far abroad, when you were within me; yet, at length, though late, I have found you, let not your mercy suffer me, O Lord, that ever I forsake or leave you again. And because to have eyes to see you is one of the chiefest things that pleases you. Lord, give me the eyes of a solitary turtle to contemplate you; give me chaste eyes full of modesty, humble and amorous, sanctified and weeping, attentive and discreet eyes which may understand and perform your will; Lord, give me grace to behold you with such eyes as you may look upon me again as you did upon Peter when he denied you and he was moved to bitter compunction for his sins. Look upon me as you did upon the prodigal child when you did run to embrace and kiss him; or as upon the publican, not daring to lift up his eyes to heaven. Behold me with those eyes that did invite Mary Magdalene to penance, and to wash your feet with tears; or, with those eyes wherewith the spouse in the Canticles incited you to her love, when you said: "How beautiful art thou, my love, how beautiful art thou! thy eyes are dove's eyes" (Song 4:1).

That my aspect be pleasing and that the beauty of my soul be grateful unto you: do you, I beseech you, bestow the gift of virtues and graces upon me, to deck and trim myself, whereby I may live to glorify your holy name for ever and ever. O merciful and holy Trinity! Father, Son, and Holy Spirit, one only true God, teach, direct, and help me in all. O Father omnipotent, I beseech you by the greatness of your immense power to confirm and strengthen my memory in you only, and to replenish it with holy and pious cogitations. O Son most wise, illuminate my small understanding with your eternal wisdom, to know your everlasting truth and my own misery. O Holy Spirit, love of the Father and the Son, with your incomprehensible goodness, make my will conformable to your divine pleasure, inflame it with such a fire of your holy love that no waters which rise from the turbulent fear of evil suggestions may be able to extinguish it. O holy Trinity and one God: I would to God I could do nothing else but praise and love you, and as much as all your holy saints; I would to God I had the love of all creatures in me alone; I would, with a willing mind transfer and turn it to the love of you, although this were nothing in respect of what you deserve. Only you yourself can worthily love and praise yourself, because none else besides you is able to understand your incomprehensible goodness, and therefore the just poise of love resides only in your sacred breast.

O Blessed Virgin Mary, Mother of God, Queen of heaven, lady of the world, mansion of the Holy Spirit, lily of purity, rose of patience, paradise of pleasure, mirror of chastity, vessel of innocence: intercede for me, miserable banished wretch, and bestow upon me a portion of your abundant charity.

O all you saints of God, and you angelic spirits who burn with a vehement affection of your Creator, especially you seraphims who inflame both heaven and earth with love, do not forsake my miserable soul, but purify it as you did the lips of Isaiah from all vice and uncleanness and set it on fire with the flames of your ardent love, that I may

love and seek our Lord God, resting and remaining in him forever and
ever. Amen.

COUNSELS FOR MEDITATION

Now we will briefly handle those things which pertain to the form and method of meditation, of which, though the Holy Spirit be the principal master, nevertheless, experience teaches us that certain counsels are likewise necessary: because the way to heaven is cragged, and full of difficulties, therefore is there need of a guide, without which many have gone astray a long time from the right path, or, at leastwise, have not attained to their desired end so soon as they expected.

The First Counsel—Avoid Rigidity in Method

The first counsel, therefore, is that we do not so adhere to those things which we have digested into several points and times as that we should think it a fault to fall upon other things, wherein the mind may reap more abundant fruit; for seeing devotion is the end of all those exercises, that which comes nearest to this scope is always to be accounted best; which ought not lightly, upon every occasion, to be done, but with a clear and manifest profit.

The Second Counsel—Avoid Excessive Intellectual Speculation

We must be wary of too many speculations in this exercise, and use rather efficacious affections of the will than curious discourses of the understanding: wherefore, they go not in the right way that meditate of divine mysteries as though they were to preach them to the people in a sermon, which is rather to dissipate than to recollect the spirit, and to wander abroad than to be busied in their own home. Therefore, he that will meditate with fruit to his soul must come to it like a humble simple creature, bringing rather a will disposed to taste these holy mysteries profitably than acrimony of understanding to discuss them learnedly; for this is proper to those who give themselves to study, not to those who consecrate themselves unto devotion.

The Third Counsel—Avoid Contrived Devotion

In the preceding counsel, we declared how the understanding is to be moderated and subjected to the will; now we will prefix some limits to the will, out of which she cannot deviate without fault. That, therefore, she be not too immoderate in her exercise, we must know that devotion is never to be secured by sheer force as some do think, who with contrived sorrow do wring out tears and commiseration while they consider the torments of Jesus Christ; for this does rather dry the heart than make it capable of divine visitations (as Cassianus does excellently teach;[1] moreover, this extraordinary force often hurts the body, and by reason of the burden which this violence brings with it, the mind is left so disturbed that it fears to return again to these exercises. When experience teaches that it is the cause of so much trouble, he, therefore, that will fruitfully meditate upon the Passion of Christ, let him not be too anxious for sensible consolation, but let it suffice that he exhibits himself present to his sufferings, beholding them with a simple and quiet eye, and considering them with a tender compassionate heart, rather disposed to entertain that affection which Almighty God's mercy shall suggest, than that which shall be wrung out with violence; which, when he has done, let him not be solicitous nor sorrowful over what other things God will not give.

---

1. Cassian, *Conferences*, Bk. IX, ch. 29.

The Fourth Counsel—Avoid Excessive Efforts to Manage Distractions

Hence we may gather what attention is to be observed in prayer; wherefore, the heart must not be languishing, remiss, or dejected; but quick, attentive, and elevated to heavenly things. And as it is necessary to come to God with such attention, elevation of the mind and abstraction from sensible things, so it is no less necessary to temper sweetly this attention, that it be neither hurtful to bodily health nor impediment to extinguish devotion. For when any be so intensive to the matter they meditate upon, without any respect to their infirm nature, do oftentimes so dull their brains that they be ruined for other exercises; on the contrary, there are some, to avoid this danger, that are so remiss and lazy in their attention that easily they suffer their minds to be distracted with other idle thoughts. These two extremes, that they may be both avoided, such moderation is necessary, that the head be not weakened with too violent attention nor the thoughts permitted carelessly to wander out of supine negligence; in which thing, we must imitate a good rider upon an unruly horse, who neither holds him in too hard nor loosens the reins upon his neck, but guides him equally, that he gives not back nor go forward too speedily. So we must strive in meditation that attention be moderate, diligently resisting evil thoughts, but not violent with anxiety. We must note also that these things we here speak of are chiefly to be taken heed of in the beginning of meditation; for it often happens that those who are too violent in the beginning do flounder in the midst of meditation, as travellers making too much speed in their setting forth are tired in the midst of their journey.

The Fifth Counsel—Persevere in Aridity

Amongst all counsels this is chiefly to be observed, that when in meditation we cannot presently perceive that sweetness of devotion we expect, not, therefore, to wax timid, or leave off from the exercise begun, but patiently, with longsuffering, expect the coming of our Lord: seeing it worthy of the excellency of the Divine Majesty, the utility and base-ness of man's condition, the importance of the business we have in hand to stay awhile before the gates of his sacred palace. If he comes presently, after a little expectation, with many thanks let us with gratitude enter-tain this undeserved favour. If he makes longer delays, let us humble ourselves before him and confess that we do not deserve this grace. If he doesn't come at all, let us bear it patiently with a quiet mind and content ourselves, that we have offered ourselves with all we have unto him, for a grateful sacrifice; that we have denied our own proper wills, resigning them unto his power; that we have crucified all our inordinate appetites; that we have fought against our passions and vices; and finally, that we have performed whatsoever was in our power to be done; and although we have not worshipped him with sensible devotion, yet let it suffice us that we have worshipped him in spirit and in truth as he requires. Last of all, let us persuade ourselves that this is the most dangerous and chiefly to be feared rock of this present navigation, and the place wherein the true and faithful servants of God are tried and distinguished from infi-dels; from which, if we shall depart in safety, in all others we shall have a prosperous success.

The Sixth Counsel—Avoid Brevity in Meditation

This counsel does not much differ from the former, which, not-withstanding, is equally necessary. And this it is that the servant of God must not content himself that he has felt a little sensible consolation from meditation, as many do when they have shed a little dry tear, or felt a little comforting of the heart, that they have attained to the scope and end of this exercise. But they are far deceived; for even as to make the earth fruitful, one little shower which lays the dust is not sufficient, but it must have a great deal of rain, thoroughly soaked into the roots of the plants, before it can give any hopes of a fruitful year, so the abun-dance of celestial waters are necessary to our souls to make them bring forth the fruit of good works. Wherefore, we are not without cause admonished by spiritual men that we should spend as much time as we possibly can in this holy exercise, and it is better to insist some long time together, than by fits, for when the time is short, it will be almost all consumed in focusing the imagination, and recollecting the heart, and it often happens, that while we should reap the fruit of our former trouble, meditation is quite broken off!

Concerning the prefixed time for meditation, it seems to me, whatsoever is less than two hours, or an hour and a half, is too little for this exercise; because almost one hour is spent in tuning the instrument of our souls, redirecting idle and unprofitable thoughts, and recollecting the mind from temporal things; and some time, also, is necessary to spend in reaping the fruit of our prayer in the latter end. Although I cannot deny, but after some pious action, the mind is better disposed for meditation, for as dried wood quickly burns, so the mind that is well disposed is sooner kindled with this celestial fire. The morning also is the best time for meditation, because the mind is then most free from occupations and therefore can with better facility apply itself to this holy exercise. But who, by reason of the multiplicity of outward affairs, cannot spend so much time? Yet, at leastwise, let them with the poor widow in the Gospel offer up to God the small mite of their sincere affection. And no doubt but he who provides for all creatures, according to their several necessities, will graciously accept it if their culpable negligence does not deserve the contrary.

The Seventh Counsel—Yield to Divine Consolations

The seventh counsel is, that he that is visited with divine consolations in or out of prayer, ought to have a special care to spend that time, above other, with fruit unto his soul; for while this prosperous gale does blow, he will go further in his journey towards heaven, in one hour, than otherwise he has, or shall do, in many days. So did the holy Father St. Francis do, of whom St. Bonaventure writes that he had such a solicitous care of divine visitations that whensoever upon the way he was recreated with them, he would either go before or stay behind his companion awhile until he had digested this divine morsel sent unto him from heaven.[2] They who are negligent and careless to answer divine visitations are commonly chastised with this punishment from God that when they seek they will hardly find them.

The Eighth Counsel—Yield to Contemplation

The last counsel and of greatest moment is, in this exercise of prayer, we must join meditation to contemplation, seeing one is, as it were, a ladder unto the other; wherefore it is the part of meditation, with diligent attention, to consider and ponder celestial things, first one, then another, that at last some pious affection may be stirred up in the soul, like him that with a steel strikes fire out of a flint; but it is the property of contemplation, which follows meditation, to enjoy this kindled fire; that is to say, to embrace that affection which, with much labor, he sought and found, in deep silence and tranquillity of spirit, not with many discourses and speculations of the understanding, but with a pure simple relation and eye to essential reality. Hence a certain doctor says that meditation does discourse with labor and small profit, but contemplation without any trouble and with much fruit; the one does seek and the other finds; the one chews and the other eats the meat; the one reasons and considers, the other contemplates those things she loves and tastes; and, in fine, the one is the means, the other is the end; the one is the way and motion, the other the term of the way and end of the action. From these things which we have said, that rule or axiom is very frequent among spiritual masters, which few of their scholars do rightly understand, that is, the end being attained unto, all means do cease. For example, the mariner rests when he comes to his desired haven.

So he that meditates, when, by the means of meditation, he shall come to the rest and sweet gust of contemplation, ought to leave the cragged way of reasoning and discourse, contenting himself with the

---

2. St. Bonaventure, *The Major Legend of St. Francis*, ch. 10, par. 2.

memory of Almighty God alone; whom he may behold as present to his soul and quietly enjoy that sweet affection which he shall generously desire to bestow upon him, whether it be of love, admiration, joy, or the like; and the reason is, because the end of this business consists rather in love and affection of the will than in speculations of the understanding. When, therefore, the will has captivated the one and attained to the other affection, all reasoning and speculations of the understanding are to be left, that the soul may bend all her forces to it without a confused wandering to the actions of the other powers. Therefore, a certain doctor gives this counsel to those who perceive themselves to be inflamed with the fire of divine love that they should quite abolish all other thoughts and speculations, never so sublime and subtle; not that they are evil, but because for the present, they hinder a greater good. And this is no other than, after we have come to the end, to leave meditation for the love of contemplation which we may do (to speak particularly of this matter) in the end of every exercise, (that is to say) after the petition of divine love, as above said, and that for two reasons: first, because it is supposed that the labor of the finished exercise has produced some fruit of devotion towards Almighty God, as the wise man says, "Better is the end of prayer, than the beginning."

Secondly, it is expedient that, after labor in prayer, the understanding rest awhile and recreate itself in the arms of contemplation. Here let everyone resist whatsoever imaginations shall present themselves unto his mind, let him still his understanding, let him fasten his memory strongly upon God, considering that he is placed in his holy presence. But let him not adhere to any particular contemplation of God, but only content himself with that knowledge which faith has ministered unto him; and to this, let him add his will and affection, seeing this is only that which embraces God, and in which the whole fruit of meditation consists. The weak understanding is little able to conceive or comprehend anything of God, but the will can love him very much.

Let him, therefore, rouse up himself from temporal things, and let him recollect himself within himself, that is to say, to the centre of his soul, where is the lively image of God; here let him hearken attentively, as though he heard Almighty God speaking from a high turret; or as though he held him fast, being present in his soul; or as though there were no other persons in the world, besides God and himself. Nay, I say more, let him quite forget himself, and those things which he does; for, as one of the ancient holy fathers says, prayer is then every way complete, when he that prays does not consider that he is before God in prayer, and this is to be done, not only in the end of the exercise, but in the midst, and in every part of meditation. For, as often as this spiritual sleep shall sweetly oppress anyone, that is to say, when the understanding is drowned as it were in a sleep, (but the will watching) let him quietly enjoy this delicate meat as long as it shall last. But when it is digested, let him return again to meditation, in which we must behave ourselves like a gardener who, when he waters a bed of his garden, after he has once sprinkled it with water, waits awhile until it be drunk in, then sprinkles again, that at last it may thoroughly wet the earth, that it may become more fruitful. But what the soul, cast into this heavenly sleep and illuminated with the splendour of this eternal light does enjoy—what satiety! what charity! what internal peace!—no tongue is able to express. This is that peace which surpasses all understanding; this is that felicity, greater than which cannot be imagined in this vale of misery.

There are many so inflamed with this fire of divine love that their interiors, at the very memory of this blessed name, without any meditation at all before, do rest in joy. These need no more consideration or discourses to love God than a mother needs motives to love her child or the bride her husband. Others there are so absorbed in God, not only in prayer but also in outward business, that they wholly forget themselves and all creatures for the love of him. Neither are these effects of divine love to be admired, seeing worldly love causes oftentimes greater matters in the minds of men that it makes them mad. What, shall we attribute less efficacy to grace than unto nature and sin? When, therefore, the soul shall feel this operation of divine love, in what part of prayer soever it happens, let him never refuse it; although he spent all the time of this exercise in it, without any manner of consideration at all, for that point he purposed to meditate upon (except he be specially obliged unto it) for, as St. Augustine says, vocal prayer ought to be left if it hinders devotion, so, meditation ought to be deferred if it hinders contemplation. But as it is necessary to leave meditation for this affection and to ascend from the lesser to the greater, so, oftentimes, this contemplation is to be left for meditation, when it is so vehement that the corporal health receives some damage thereby. This oftentimes happens to those who, taken with the pleasure of this divine sweetness, give themselves too indiscreetly to these exercises, and use them too immoderately, to whom (as a certain doctor saith) this will be the best remedy: that they desist from contemplation, turning their minds to some other good affection, as of compassion in meditating on the sufferings of our Savior, or about the sins and miseries of this world, to exonerate the heart, diverting it from that too much intension.

DEEPENING DEVOTION

What is Devotion?

Devotion makes all things easy: Amongst all the troublesome difficulties to which they who frequent the exercises of prayer and meditation are subject, none is greater than that which they suffer from the defect of devotion which often is felt in prayer. For if they have this, nothing is more sweet, nothing more pleasant, nothing more easy than to insist on prayer and meditation. But if that be wanting, nothing more hard, nothing more difficult, nothing more burdensome than to pray. Wherefore, seeing we have already spoken of prayer, meditation, and the method to perform it, now it will not be beside our purpose to treat of those things which partly promote and partly hinder and extinguish devotion in the mind of man; as also to lay open the temptations which are obvious to those who frequent these pious exercises; and, last of all, to annex some certain counsels which may not a little avail to the well performance of this business. We will, therefore, begin from the definition of devotion, that it may manifestly appear what a precious pearl it is for which we war.

Devotion, as St. Thomas says, is a virtue which makes a man prompt and ready to every virtuous deed and stirring him up to do well; which definition evidently shows the necessity and utility of this virtue, as containing more in it than any man can imagine. For the better understanding of this, we must know that the chief impediment that hinders us from leading a virtuous life is the corruption of human nature proceeding from sin, which brings with it a vehement inclination to vice and a great difficulty to do well; this makes the way of virtue cragged and troublesome, although in itself considered, nothing in this world is so sweet, so lovely, so beautiful. The divine wisdom has ordained the help of devotion as a most convenient remedy to overcome this difficulty; for, as the north wind dissipates clouds and makes a clear sky, so true devotion expels from the mind the tediousness of this way and makes us with alacrity prompt to pious actions. This virtue does so far forth obtain the name of virtue that likewise it is a special gift of the Holy Spirit: a heavenly dew, an assistance obtained by prayer whose property is to remove all difficulties happening in prayer and meditation, to expel tepidity, to minister alacrity in the divine service, to instruct the understanding, to strengthen the will, to kindle in our hearts heavenly love, to extinguish the flames of unlawful desires, to engender a hatred and loathing of sin and all transitory things, and, last of all, to him that possesses it, to infuse a new fervor, a new spirit, a new mind, and new desires to do well. For, as Samson, as long as he had his hair, did exceed all men in strength, but when that was cut, he was weak as others; so the soul of every Christian, recreated with the help of devotion, is strong and valiant. But when it is deprived of it, it becomes infirm and weak. But, above all the praises which can be heaped upon this virtue, this is the chief, that although it be but only one virtue, yet it is a prick and motive to all. They, therefore, that desire to walk in a virtuous way, must get this for a spur, for without it, he will never be able to rule his rebellious flesh.

In what devotion consists: Hence, it manifestly appears, in what the essence of devotion consists, not in tenderness of heart or abundance of consolations, wherewith they who meditate are often recreated, except a prompt cheerful readiness of the mind to do well be thereunto adjoined; especially, seeing it sometimes happens the one to be found without the other, Almighty God so disposing for the trial of his servants. Though I cannot deny but that these consolations do often proceed from devotion and promptitude of the mind to do well and, on the contrary, that true devotion is not a little augmented by the same consolations and spiritual consolations; and, therefore, the servants of God may lawfully desire and ask them, not for the delight they bring with them but because they do greatly increase devotion which makes us, with cheerful readiness, to apply ourselves to virtuous actions which the kingly prophet testifies himself saying, "I have run the ways of thy commandments when thou hast enlarged my heart," that is, when you have recreated me with the sweetness of your consolations, which are the cause of this my readiness.

Now let us treat of the means whereby this virtue is to be attained unto, which will bring no small profit with it, for seeing it is the spur to all other virtues, to set down the means whereby it is to be obtained is no other thing than to prescribe the means to get all other virtues.

Nine Means to Acquire Devotion

The things which promote devotion are many, of which we will handle a few.

Completion of the exercise: First, it helps much devotion if those exercises be undertaken with a generous resolution, ready to undergo whatever difficulty shall occur for the obtaining of this precious pearl. For it is certain that nothing is excellent which is not difficult, of which kind is devotion, especially in beginnings.

Custody of the heart: Secondly, a diligent custody of the heart from every vain and unprofitable consideration, from affections, strange love, and turbulent motions, does much promote devotion. For it is evident that every one of these is no little hindrance, seeing this virtue chiefly requires a quiet heart, free from all inordinate affection and so well composed as the strings of a well-tuned instrument.

Custody of the senses: Thirdly, custody of the senses, especially the eyes, tongue, and ears, seeing by these, the heart is much distracted. For those things which enter in through the eyes and ears do strain the mind with divers imaginations and consequently disturb and trouble the peace and tranquillity of the soul. Wherefore, one not without cause said that he that meditates must be deaf, blind, and dumb; for by how much less he wanders abroad, with greater recollection will he rejoice at home.

Solitude: Fourthly, solitude helps devotion much, for it does not only remove the occasions of sin, and take away the causes which chiefly disturb the heart and senses, but it makes a solitary man to rouse up himself from temporal things, to be present to himself and converse incessantly with God. To which, the opportunity of the place does admonish which admits no other society.

Reading of spiritual books: Fifthly, the reading of spiritual books does not a little nourish devotion, because it provides profitable matter for consideration, lifts the mind above all things created, stirs up devotion, and causes a man to sooner adhere to the consideration of those things which, in reading, offered him a more pleasant taste than wherewith the heart abounds and that they may more frequently occur to his memory.

Continual memory of God: Sixthly, continual memory of Almighty God and daily imagination of his sacred presence, that always you are in his sight, with a frequent use of aspirations, which St. Augustine calls ejaculatory prayers; for these do guard the palace of the mind, conserving devotion in her fervor, that a man is always willing to pious actions and ready to holy prayer. This counsel is one of the principal instruments of a spiritual life and the only remedy for those who have neither time nor place with opportunity to insist to long prayer and meditation; and they which do thus bestow their labor to frequent aspirations will, in a short time, profit much.

Perseverance: Seventhly, perseverance in good exercises, that so times and places be duly observed, especially morning and evening, as fittest times for prayer.

Corporal austerities: Eighthly, corporal abstinence and corporal austerities do much help devotion, fasting from meat, a frugal table, a hard bed, hair cloth, discipline, and the like. As they originally proceed from devotion of the mind, so they do not a little cherish, conserve, and nourish the root from whence they spring, which is devotion.

Works of mercy: Lastly, works of mercy are a great spur to devotion, because they increase the confidence we have to appear before God and to be presented before his sacred Majesty. They do accompany our prayers; and, finally, they merit that they be sooner heard by God, especially seeing they proceed from a merciful heart.

Nine Impediments to Devotion

As there be nine things which do promote devotion, so likewise there be nine impediments that do hinder the same.

Venial sins: The first impediment of devotion is sins not only mortal, but also venial, for these, although they do not quite abolish charity, yet, at leastwise they diminish the fervor of it and consequently make us less apt to devotion. Wherefore, with all diligence they are to be avoided, not only for the evil they bring with them, but also for the good which they hinder.

Remorse of conscience: Secondly, excessive remorse of conscience proceeding from sins, when it is in extremes, because it does disquiet the mind, weakens the head, and makes a man unfit for acts of virtue.

Anxiety of heart: Thirdly, anxiety of heart and inordinate sadness, for with these, the heart, delights of a good conscience, and spiritual joy of the inward mind, can hardly suit and agree.

Cares of the mind: Fourthly, too many cares which do disquiet the mind, like the Egyptian prefects who did oppress the children of Israel with too immoderate labors, nor will ever suffer them to take that spiritual repose which they should have often had in prayer. Yea, at that time, above others, they disturb the mind, endeavoring to seduce her from her spiritual exercise.

A multitude of affairs: Fifthly, a multitude of activities which take up our whole time suffocates the spirit, scarcely leaving for a man a moment to employ in Almighty God's service.

Delights and pleasures of the senses: Sixthly, delights and pleasures of the senses, for these make spiritual exercises unappealing and a man unworthy to be recreated with heavenly consolations; for, as St. Bernard says, he is not worthy of the visitations of the Holy Spirit, that seeks after consolation in the pleasures of the world.

Inordinate eating and drinking: Seventhly, inordinate delight in eating and drinking: especially long eating and sumptuous suppers, which make a man unapt to spiritual exercises. For when the body is oriented to excessive pampering, the spirit cannot so freely elevate itself to God.

Curiosity of the senses and understanding: Eighthly, curiosity of the senses and understanding, as to see sights and hear of the new rumors, because these do spend precious time, disturb and overthrow the tranquillity of the mind, distracting it with many impertinences which can be no small hindrance to devotion.

Intermission of exercises: Lastly, a laxity in spiritual exercises, except when they are not omitted or deferred for a pious cause or just necessity. For the spirit of devotion is delicate, which, when it is gone, it hardly returns again, at least with great difficulty. For as trees and plants must be watered in due season, otherwise they wither away and perish, so devotion, except it be watered with the waters of holy meditation, does easily vanish.

These things we have set down briefly, that they may be the better remembered; use and experience of them will afford a longer explication.

COMMON TEMPTATIONS IN MEDITATION AND THEIR REMEDIES

Now, let us see with what temptations they, who frequent the exercise of prayer and meditation, are molested, that we may provide convenient remedies for them, which be these:

- First, the lack of spiritual consolations.
- Second, a multitude of unprofitable thoughts.
- Third, thoughts of infidelity and blasphemy.
- Fourth, fancies in the night.
- Fifth, sleepiness and drowsiness.
- Sixth, timidity or fear of advancing.
- Seventh, too much presumption of their own sanctity.
- Eighth, inordinate desire of learning.
- Ninth, indiscreet zeal.

These are the common temptations which do trouble those who lead a virtuous life.

A Remedy for the First Temptation—Dryness of Spirit

What to do in the time of dryness of spirit: To him that lacks spiritual consolations, this is the remedy, that therefore he remains constant in his customary exercises of prayer, although they seem difficult and appear to bear little fruit; but let him set himself in the presence of

God, coming before him as guilty of many grievous sins; let him search, diligently, the corners of his own conscience and consider whether or not through his own fault he has lost this grace; if so, let him beseech Almighty God to pardon him for this sin, admiring the inestimable riches of his divine patience in tolerating us so long.

The reward of those who in the time of dryness of spirit do not leave off their wonted exercise: By this means he will reap no small fruit from his aridity of spirit, taking from thence occasion of deeper humility, when he considers his own malice and perverseness in heaping up of sin, or of more ardent affection, when he sees Almighty God's goodness in pardoning the same. And, although he enjoys no pleasure at all in his exercises, let him not, therefore, abstain from the continuation of them, for it is not always necessary that it should be sweet and savory to the present taste, which will be hereafter profitable. Especially when it is often seen by experience that those who constantly persevere in their intended exercises, not giving over in the time of this aridity, but continue them with what care and diligence possibly they are able, that these, I say, depart from this table recreated with many heavenly consolations and much spiritual joy, seeing they find nothing to be omitted on their parts. It is but a small matter to protract prayer for a long space when it flows with consolations, but when these are taken away, not to desist is an admirable act of virtue; for in this humility emerges, patience is eminent and true perseverance in good works is manifested.

But it is necessary in the time of aridity to have a greater care of himself, watching over himself with greater diligence, to discuss his conscience more sincerely, and to observe all his words and actions more accurately. For then, when alacrity and spiritual joy (which is the principal oar of his navigation) is absent, with greater vigilance the defect of grace is to be supplied. When you find yourself to be in this state, you ought to think, as St. Bernard admonishes, that the sentinels which did watch you are asleep, that the walls that did defend you are broken down, and therefore, the only hope of safeguard to consist in arms.

When all is gone which did otherwise protect you, safety is to be sought with an armed hand. O what deserved glory follows such a soul which wins the triumphant laurel after such a manner, she fights a combat with the enemy, without either sword or buckler, is valiant without help, who, although she be alone, sustains the whole battle with as much courage as though she were surrounded with troops of auxiliary forces. This perseverance is the chiefest proof, whereby the sincerity and goodness of the friends of God is known, whereby the true are separated from false servants.

A Remedy for the Second Temptation—Unprofitable Thoughts

What to do when we have unprofitable thoughts: Against the temptation of importune and unprofitable cogitations which are wont to trouble those that pray and disquiet them with no small disturbance, this is the remedy: to resist them manfully, provided always the resistance be not joined with too much violence and anxiety of spirit. Seeing this work depends not so much on our strength, as Almighty God's grace and profound humility, wherefore, when anyone is beset with these temptations, let him confidently turn himself to God without any scruple or anxiety of mind, (seeing this is no fault, or at least, a very small one,) with great submission and devotion of heart, saying, "behold, Lord, behold what I am! What other thing can be looked for from this disgusting odor, but such filthy savors? What other fruit can be expected from this earth, which you cursed in the beginning of the world, but thorns and thistles? What good can it bring forth, except you Lord, purge it from all corruption?" This being said, let him return to continue his meditations with patience, expecting the visitation of our Lord, who is never wanting to the humble of spirit.

If yet the tumult of these troublesome fancies does not cease, nevertheless let him still resist constantly, repelling the force of them to the utmost of his power. From this perseverant battle, believe me, he will reap more gain and merit than if he had enjoyed the greatest consolations in his meditation.

A Remedy for the Third Temptation—Thoughts of Blasphemy

Temptation of thoughts of blasphemy ought to be despised: To overcome the temptation of blasphemous thoughts, we must know as there is no temptation so troublesome to a pious mind, so likewise, there is none less dangerous; therefore the best remedy is to vigorously reject them, for seeing sin consists not in sense but delight of those things we think of. But in these there is no pleasure, but rather torture; therefore, they may challenge the name of punishment rather than of sin; and the more vexation is in them, the further off we are from consenting unto any sin; therefore it is best not to fear but to confidently resist them, seeing fear makes them more strong and violent.

A Remedy for the Fourth Temptation—More on Challenging Thoughts

In considering God's works, good heed ought to be taken: Against the temptations of infidelity, he who is troubled with such obsessive thoughts on the one side, let him consider the imbecility of man's condition on the other side, the greatness of the divine power to whom nothing is impossible; those things which God has commanded, let him always bear in mind; for others, let him never busy himself in searching curiously the works of Supreme Majesty, seeing the least of them do so far transcend human capacity. Wherefore, he that desires to enter into this sanctuary of God's works, let him enter with profound humility and reverence, endued with the eyes of a simple dove, not of a subtle serpent; and let him bear the mind of a meek disciple, and not of an imprudent judge; let him put on the shape of a child, for such our Lord makes partakers of his divine secrets; let him not mind to search or know the causes of God's works; let him shut the eyes of natural reason, and open the eyes of faith, for these are the hands wherewith God's works ought to be handled. Human understanding is able to comprehend the works of men but not of God, seeing they are not capable of so much light. This temptation, seeing it is one of the greatest which assaults men, and brings none or small delight with it, is to be cured with the remedy of the precedent temptation; that is to make slight of it, for it cannot damage the soul with any great blemish, because where the will is contrary, there is no danger of any sin.

A Remedy for the Fifth Temptation—Fighting Fear

Fear is overcome with fighting not fleeing: There are some who are troubled with many fears and fancies when they go to pray in solitary places, remote from the company of men, against which temptation there is no more efficacious remedy than for a man to arm himself with a courageous mind, persevering in his exercise, for this fear is overcome with fighting not fleeing; moreover, let him consider that not the devil nor any other thing whatsoever can hurt us, except as God permits. Let him also consider that we are compassed about with a custody of angels which do guard us, as well in as out of prayer; they assist us, carrying up our prayers to heaven; they help us to bring to nothing the devices of our crafty enemy and to confound all his mischievous plots.

A Remedy for the Sixth Temptation—Drowsiness in Prayer

Drowsiness in prayer occurs from a threefold cause: To overcome sleep, wherewith some that meditate are often troubled, we must consider that sometimes it proceeds from mere necessity and then it is not to be denied the body what is its due lest it hinders what is our right. Sometimes it proceeds out of infirmity; then he must take heed not to trouble himself too much, seeing herein is no sin at all, but moderately, as much as strength suffers, resisting it; now using some industry, then some small violence, that prayer does not altogether perish, without which nothing in this life can be had secure. But when it emerges out of sloth or from the devil, then there is no better remedy than to abstain from wine and not to use water in abundance, but as much as quenches his thirst; to pray upon his knees or after some other painful gesture of the body, let him use discipline, or other corporal austerity to drive sleep from his eyes. To conclude, the remedy for this and all others is instantly to implore his assistance, who is ready to give it to all, so they ask it fervently and constantly.

A Remedy for the Seventh Temptation—Timidity and Presumption

Man ought chiefly to rely upon God's grace, not his own merits: Against the temptations of timidity and presumption, seeing that they in themselves be contrary, it is requisite to apply diverse remedies. Against timidity, let him consider that we do not rest upon our own merits but upon Almighty God's grace; who is so much the more willing to assist man, by how much the more he is humble as a result of recognizing the limits of his own capabilities, placing a firm hope in the goodness of God, to whom nothing is impossible. The remedy for presumption is to consider that the most evident and certain argument is that a man is yet furthest from true sanctity when he thinks himself to be nearest. Moreover, let him look upon himself in the lives of the saints who now reign with Christ, or live yet in this mortal life, as in a looking glass, to which of these he compares himself, he will see that he is no more than a dwarf in respect of a giant; which consideration will not a little suppress his pride.

A Remedy for the Eighth Temptation—Inordinate Draw to Study

The divine wisdom infinitely exceeds human prudence: Against the inordinate desire of study and the divine learning, it is good to consider how far the value of virtue exceeds the value of knowledge, and how much the knowledge of God dwarfs human wisdom. Hence a man may learn how necessary it is to bestow more labor upon one than upon the other. Moreover, the world has all the excellence that can be desired but cannot avoid this misery: that it must end with life. What then is more miserable than to seek after that, with so much labor and expense, which so quickly perishes? If all things in the world could be known, they are but as nothing; and, therefore, it is much better to exercise ourselves in the love of God, the fruit whereof remains for ever, and in whom we see and know all things. Last of all, in the day of judgment we shall not be asked what we have read, but what we have done; not how eloquently we have spoken, but how well we have lived.

A Remedy for the Ninth Temptation—Indiscreet Zeal for Activity

The salvation of our neighbor is so to be regarded that we do not neglect our own: The chiefest remedy against indiscreet zeal of helping others is so to attend to the good of our neighbors in a way that we take care not to neglect our prayer and devotion. And so to have a care of the consciences of others, that we neglect not our own; but in assisting them, it is good to reserve so much time as is sufficient to conserve the heart in devotion and recollection. And this is, as St. Paul saith: "To walk in spirit," that is to say, that a man be more in God than in himself. Seeing, therefore, that the prime root of all our good upon this depends, we must strive that our prayer be so profound and long as may conserve the soul in devotion, which every short meditation is not able to do, but devout and long meditation.

OTHER CERTAIN ADMONITIONS NECESSARY FOR SPIRITUAL PERSONS

The First Admonition—On the Pursuit of Consolations

The error and abuse of some: The thing that affords greatest difficulty in this spiritual journey is to know how to come to God and to converse with him familiarly. Let, therefore, none dare to enter in this way without a good guide, and well instructed with necessary admonitions and counsels, of which we will set down a few, according to our wonted brevity.

The first is whereby we are taught what end we must aim at in these our spiritual exercises. We must therefore know that since to communicate with Almighty God of itself is most delightful, having no bitterness mixed with it, as the wise man testifies: hence it comes to pass that many, allured with the pleasure of this admirable and unused sweetness (which is greater than can be comprehended) come to God, and frequent these spiritual actions, as reading, prayer, meditation, use of the Sacrament, for the great content and delight they take in them, so that for the principal end, wherewith they are moved, is this admirable sweetness which they vehemently desire. This is a grave error, and many are plunged into it; for seeing to love and seek God should be the chiefest end of all our actions, these love and seek themselves; that is to say, their own gust and sensible delight rather than God, which was the scope of the contemplative philosophy of the gentiles; especially as a certain doctor saith, that this is a kind of avarice, luxury, and spiritual gluttony, no less pernicious than carnal. From this error springs another branch: to wit, that many judge themselves and others, according to the ebbing and flowing of consolations, so far that they are persuaded that a man is more or less perfect by how much more or less he is visited with divine consolations. This is a great mistake.

What should be the end of our spiritual exercises: Against both these temptations, this general doctrine is a remedy: that everyone must know the scope of all these exercises and the chief end of a spiritual life is the observing of God's commandments and a perfect fulfilling of his divine will; to this it is necessary that our own will be mortified, that the will of God may the better live and reign in us, seeing both these are directly contrary the one to the other. But this noble victory, seeing it cannot be obtained without special favor and allurements of God, therefore we ought to frequent the exercise of prayer, the better by it (and indeed the only means) to obtain this grace and to bring this serious business of our soul's perfection to a good and desired end. With this intention we may confidently desire of God internal consolation, as we have said before. This did the prophet David, when he said: "Give me, O Lord, the joy of your salvation, and confirm me with your principal spirit."

Hence it is manifest what end everyone ought to prefix to himself in these exercises, and how they should esteem and measure their own and other's profit; not according to the multitude of flowing consolations, but according to those things they have constantly suffered for God, partly in fulfilling his divine pleasure, partly in renouncing their own proper wills. And that this ought to be the end of all our prayer and reading, it appears by that one psalm of the prophet David which begins, "Blessed are the immaculate in the way, which walk in the law of the Lord" which is the longest psalm in the psalter, notwithstanding, there is not one verse in it in which there is not mention of the law of God and keeping his commandments, which the Holy Spirit has so ordained, that men may learn to direct all prayer and reading to this end and scope. From which they that do decline cast themselves into the secret snares of the enemy, who with his subtle craft persuades them, that is, some great matter which, indeed, is nothing; and for this cause men, most exercised in spiritual matters, do affirm the only touchstone of true virtue to be not that sensible delight which is found in prayer, but patience in affliction, abnegation of one's self, a sincere and entire fulfilling of the divine will, and, finally, in a diligent observing of Almighty God's laws and commandments; though I must confess that prayer itself and the frequent consolations that are found therein, do not a little conduce and help to the better effecting of these things before mentioned.

They who are desirous to know how much progress they have made in the way of God, let them examine how much they have increased in interior and exterior humility; how willingly they have put up with injuries; with what mind they have borne with others' infirmities; how they have patiently absorbed the imperfections of their neighbors; what confidence they have had in God, in the tedious time of tribulation; how they have bridled their tongues; how they have kept their heart; how they have mortified their flesh, and made it subject to the spirit; with what moderation they have behaved themselves in prosperity and adversity; with what gravity and discretion they have governed all their actions; and, above all, how dead they have been to the world with all its pleasures, honors, and dignities; and accordingly as they have profited in these virtues, let them measure their perfection and not according to the consolations wherewith God has visited them. Wherefore, let everyone be sure to bear one hand and the chiefest over himself in mortification, the other in prayer, seeing the one cannot be attained unto without the other.

The Second Admonition—On Rejecting Spiritual Experiences

As it is inappropriate to desire consolations and spiritual comforts, to that end that in them we should set up our rest, but only as they assist us in our spiritual progress, much less is it lawful to wish for visions, revelations, and the like; which to those who are not well grounded in humility may be a great cause of their utter ruin. Neither is there any reason to fear that those who refuse or reject them should be disobedient to God; because when it shall please God to reveal anything, he will do it after such a fashion that he to whom such things shall be revealed shall be so certain of them that he will have no reason either to fear or doubt, though he should himself never so much strive against them.

The Third Admonition—On Revealing Spiritual Consolations to Others

We must have a special care not to speak to others of those sensible consolations which Almighty God has been pleased to recreate us with, except it be to our spiritual director. Hence it is, that that wise Doctor was wont to advise everyone to have these words written in great letters in his chamber: "My secret to myself, my secret to myself."[1]

The Fourth Admonition—On Humility

Moreover we must always take good heed to deal with God with much humility and reverence, never to esteem ourselves so high in his favor as to neglect to cast down our eyes upon our own baseness and to shroud our wings in the presence of so great a majesty, as holy Augustine was wont to do, of whom it is written that he had learned to rejoice before God with fear and trembling.

---

1. Sermon 23, *On the Song of Songs: Isaiah* 24:16.

The Fifth Admonition—On Dedication to Prayer

We have heretofore counselled the servant of God that he consecrates some certain time of the day to recollection. But now besides the ordinary course, we say that he must sometimes sequester himself from all business and employments, as much as is possible, and give himself wholly over to devotion, the better to nourish his soul with the abundance of spiritual consolations, recovering his daily losses and getting new force to go forward in his spiritual journey. Which, although it be not amiss to do at all times, yet more specially upon the principal feasts of the year, in the time of temptation, after a long journey, after troublesome business which gave matter of much distraction, that when we exclude from our souls all exterior things and call ourselves back again to the point from whence we did digress.

The Sixth Admonition—On Spiritual Gluttony

There be many who, gluttonous in their spiritual exercises, when they enjoy heavenly consolations, it oftentimes falls out that this prosperity exposes them to manifest peril, for when Almighty God showers down more abundantly this celestial dew upon their souls, they are so ravished with the sweetness of it that they addict themselves without measure to this only exercise; to this end they prolong the time of prayer, macerate themselves with watching and other corporal austerities so that nature itself, at length, is constrained to sink under the burden of such indiscreet mortification.

Hence it comes to pass that many abhor spiritual exercises, and some are not only made by this means unfit for corporal but also dull for spiritual labors of prayer and meditation. Wherefore, in all these there is great need of discretion, especially in the beginning when spiritual consolations be more fervent and commonly when discretion is least, for we must so order our diet that we do not faint in the midst of our journey. On the contrary, there be some so slothful and undevout that under the color of discretion, immoderately make much of themselves, refusing the least labor or trouble. This is dangerous to all, but especially to beginners; for as St. Bernard says, it is impossible that he should persevere long in a spiritual course who is indiscreet at first. That when he is a novice esteems himself wise and when he is young governs himself like an old man. Neither can I easily judge which of these be more dangerous, except as Thomas à Kempis says, the first is more incurable, for while the body is strong and sound, there may be hopes to cure tepidity; but when it is once weakened through indiscretion, it scarce ever can be brought to its former fervor.

The Seventh Admonition—On the Error of Prayer Alone

There is yet another danger more pernicious than the former, which is that some having experience of this inestimable virtue of prayer, think that all the fruit of a spiritual life depends upon it. Hence they persuade themselves, that in it all is contained and that only personal prayer is necessary for our salvation, which makes them to neglect other virtues which are likewise the foundations and pillars which do uphold a spiritual building, which being taken away the whole fabric falls to ruin; wherefore, they that seek after this one only virtue with such indiscreet fervor, the more they labor the less fruit they reap. But the servant of God that expects merit and comfort in the way of perfection must not fix his eyes so much upon one only virtue, although it be never so rare and excellent, but generally attend to all, as one string upon an instrument makes no music except we strike the rest, so one virtue cannot make a spiritual harmony in our souls if the other be wanting, not unlike a clock, which if there be but a fault in one wheel, the others will stand; so it is in a spiritual clock, if one virtue be deficient.

The Eighth Admonition—On Legalism

These things which we have hitherto said, which do help to devotion, are so to be taken himself to Almighty God's grace and behave himself manfully in his holy service, with this caution, that we should not put our confidence in them, but in God. This I say because there are some who work to reduce authentic devotion to following a set of rules, thinking that they have attained to the perfection of that exercise if they observe exactly the rules thereof.

But they who put good principles into practice will quickly attain unto their desired end, which doing, they are not to reduce grace to human agency, nor to attribute that to human rules which is the gift of God. Hence we say that it is not necessary to follow these rules and counsels as depending on human agency, but as instruments of grace; because a man will learn thus to know that the principal means by which one ought to seek after is profound humility, with the consideration of our own baseness and a great confidence in Almighty God's mercy. To the end that we may come to the knowledge of the one and the other, let us pour out tears without intermission and continually pray, that as we expectantly wait at the gate of humility, so we may obtain by it all our desires and persevere in humble thanksgiving to the divine bounty, without any trust to our own works or to anything that is ours.

The Subject Matter of Prayer and Daily Meditations

Having taken notice of the utility of prayer and meditation, we will now declare the matter about which meditation is to be conversant; for seeing it is ordained to this end that the soul of him that meditates may be excited to the fear and love of God and the keeping of his commandments, the matter of meditation ought to be such as does next dispose to this end, and scope. And, although every creature and the whole Scripture itself be able to minister this matter unto us, yet speaking generally, the mysteries of our holy faith contained in the Creed are most efficacious and profitable to attain unto this end. For these on the one side contain Almighty God's benefits, the latter judgment, the pains of hell and the glory of paradise; all which, like sharp pricks do spur us on to the love and fear of God. On the other side, they comprehend the life and Passion of our Lord and Savior, which is the spring and fountain of all our good.

These two things contained in the Apostles' Creed, for the most part yield matter of meditation; and therefore, I think, prayer and meditation ought chiefly to be conversant about them, although every one in particular may have certain points, which may more specially inflame and excite the soul to the love and fear of God. Being, therefore, persuaded with this reason, that I might the better conduct young beginners and untrained soldiers into this way of mental prayer and that I might give unto them altogether prepared and (as it were to little children) foreshowed matter of meditation, I have selected two kinds of meditations, almost taken out of the mysteries of our faith, the one serving for the morning, the other for the evening; that as the body is commonly fed with two meals, so the soul may be strengthened and nourished with two spiritual reflections, by the meditation and consideration of heavenly things. Some of these are of the Passion and Resurrection of our Lord Jesus Christ, others of the mysteries of our faith, as I said before. But those who do not have the opportunity to meditate twice a day after this manner, they may use them, to wit, they may take to their consideration the seven former meditations in the one week and the latter in another week; or they may chiefly insist upon those of the life and Passion of our Savior; although the other be not to be neglected, especially in the beginning of a soul's conversion, to whom they are proper, when the fear of God, contrition, and horror of sin is chiefly to be regarded and sought after.

Summary of Meditation Elements

To aid the reader we have here repeated St. Peter's six elements of meditation to be utilized with the daily meditations that follow.

Preparation: First, before we apply ourselves to meditation, it is necessary that our mind and soul be diligently prepared for this holy exercise; as the strings of an instrument, except they be beforehand well tuned, will never make a pleasant melody.

Reading: After preparation ought to follow the reading of some holy mystery, according to the distribution of days in the week, which in young beginners is chiefly necessary until with continual use and custom matter of meditation offers itself unto their memories.

Meditation, Giving of Thanks, Oblation: Then insist upon the matter to be meditated upon. To meditation we must join devout and sincere giving of thanks to God for all his benefits; then a general oblation of all the life of Christ for recompense of any benefit and our own works to the honor and glory of God.

Petition: Last of all, petition, which is chiefly called prayer, wherein we desire all things necessary for our own salvation, of our neighbours and the good of the whole Church.

Seven Meditations

A Meditation for Monday—On Sin and Self-Knowledge

This day you shall call to memory your sins, pursue self knowl edge; that on the one hand you may truly ponder the greatness of your offenses, and on the other hand, you may look into your baseness and nothingness and acknowledge that all the good which you have is from God. This consideration will profit you with godly thinking and true humility, the mother of all virtues. First, therefore, carefully consider the multitude of the sins of your former life, and namely those sins which you had committed when as yet you were not illuminated with the divine splendor to know Almighty God rightly. If you examine your failures with exquisite diligence, you will find them to be so many in number that they will exceed the hairs of your head; for in this time you led the life of a heathen, ignorant of the divine power and, as it were, without any knowledge of his sacred Deity. Then consider how you have behaved yourself about the Ten Commandments and the seven deadly sins and you will find that there is no precept of Almighty God which you have not violated, nor any mortal sin into which you have not fall-en, either in thought, word, or deed.

After that, call to mind Almighty God's benefits, which he has bestowed upon you in the whole course of your former life, and see whether you can give a good account of them or not. Tell me, I pray you, how have you spent the days of your infancy, youth, and the flower of your adult age? How have you employed your five exterior senses and inward faculties of your soul given to you by God, only to be busied about his holy service and the contemplation of heavenly things? What have you turned your eyes unto, but to behold vanities? What have your ears listened after, but lies and tales? What has your tongue uttered, but murmurings and blasphemous speeches? What has your taste and feeling delighted in, but wanton pleasures? How have you used the remedy of the holy Sacraments, given to you as a singular gift? What thanksgiving have you given for so many benefits which he has heaped upon you? What eagerness have you employed to pursue his holy inspirations? How have you spent your health of body and natural forces? How have you dispensed your goods of fortune? What good use have you made of the commodity and proffered occasions to live well? What care have you had of your neighbor's welfare? What works of mercy or of bounty have you done unto them? What will you answer in that terrible day of judgment when you must render a severe account of all these things?! O withered tree, destined to eternal flames, except you do penance! What excuse will you then frame when you must give an account of every year, of every month, of every week, of every day, of every moment!

Thirdly, consider, those sins, which you have every day committed, after Almighty God has illuminated and opened the eyes of your soul to meditate upon heavenly things; and you will find that the old Adam has yet borne a great sway in your action and that sinful root to have procreated in you many and perverse habits. Diligently ponder how ungrateful you have been to Almighty God, how unmindful of his benefits, how contrary you have behaved yourself against his holy inspirations, how slothful and remiss in his divine service; in which you scarce have ever used due alacrity and diligence or such purity of intention as is requisite, nay, have you not served God for worldly respects and commodity? Enter into consideration of how rigid you are toward your neighbor and how indulgent to yourself? How you love your own will; how you adhere to your sensuality; how careful of your own honor and of everything that belongs to you. Weigh well with yourself: how every day you grow more arrogant, more ambitious, more vain, more prone to anger, more desperately bent to malice, more prone to delights and pleasures, more mutable, more unconstant, more propense to carnal sins and a greater lover of earthly vanities.

Consider your inconstancy in good, your indiscretion in words, imprudence in deeds, in high and difficult matters cowardice sometimes, and often audacious temerity. In the fourth place, after you have taken notice of the number and order of your sins, pause upon them a while in your mind and weigh every one in the balance of due consideration that you may perceive with what misery you have on every side embraced.

Which, that you may the better do, consider these three circumstances in the sins of your former life. First, against whom you have sinned. Second, why you have sinned. Third, how you have sinned. Which, if you diligently penetrate, you will find that you have offended God whose majesty and goodness is immense, who has obliged man unto him with so many benefits as there are sands in the sea or drops of water in the ocean. Why have you sinned, or what violent occasion has forced you to any crime? A little momentary pride, a foul representation of pleasure, some small commodity placed in your sight, and oftentimes no occasion at all, but evil custom and mere contempt of God.

But alas, how have you sinned? With such facility, with such notable audacity, with so little fear and conscience, yea with such serenity and pleasure, as though you had to do with no other than a wooden God, who regards not these sublunary things, neither understands nor sees anything which is done on the face of earth. Is this the honor due unto his supreme majesty? Is this a remuneration of his benefits? Do you with such services requite his whippings, his buffetings, and his precious blood shed upon the Cross for your sake? O wicked wretch, that have offended so great a majesty, more miserable, that for so slight a cause, and most deplorable that you are not sensible of your utter ruin, that after sin you fear not damnation and so neglect to do penance. Moreover, it is very profitable to insist a while upon this consideration and that you esteem yourself nothing and certainly persuade yourself that you have nothing of yourself but sin; all other things to be the gifts of Almighty God's bounty. For it is most evident that all our good, both of grace and nature, does flow from him; for he is the author of the grace of predestination (which is the fountain and original of all others), of the grace of our vocation, of concomitant and preserving grace, and of the grace of everlasting life. What have you then that you canst boast of, but sin? Only this, nothing you can attribute to yourself, all other things belong to God; whence you may clearly and manifestly perceive what he is, and what you art, and hence conjecture what diffidence you ought to have in yourself and what confidence in God, to love him, and to glorify yourself in him and not in yourself, but so far as his grace does freely operate in you.

These things being digested with attentive meditation, as much as you can, urge yourself to a contempt of yourself; imagine that you are like an empty reed, shaken with every blast of wind, without gravity, without virtue, without constancy, without stability, and, finally, without anything. Think yourself to be a Lazarus four days dead, a stinking and abominable carcass, swarming with vermin, so filthy that passers-by are forced to stop their nostrils, lest they smell such a nasty savour. Believe me, you are more abominable before God and his holy saints. Think yourself unworthy to lift up your eyes to heaven; to tread upon the earth or that the creatures should serve you; yea, not worthy to eat bread or breathe in the air. Cast yourself, with the sinful women in the Gospel, at our Blessed Savior's feet, presenting yourself unto him with a confused and blushing countenance, no otherwise than the woman taken in adultery before her husband, and with inward sorrow and true compunction, beg pardon for your sins, that, for his infinite mercy and goodness, he would vouchsafe to receive you again into his favor and that you may dwell in his house for ever.

A Meditation for Tuesday—On the Miseries of This Life

This day you will meditate upon the miseries of the life of man, out of which consideration, you will take notice of worldly vanities, and learn how much glory of them ought to be despised, seeing they are built upon so weak a foundation as our fading life, whose miseries, because they be innumerable, you will take but seven of the principles for your meditation.

First, therefore, consider the shortness of the life of man, being restrained within the limits of threescore and ten, or fourscore years; whatsoever the overplus be, it is but labor and sorrow, as the Prophet speaks. Out of this time, if you do subtract your infancy, which time you lived rather the life of a beast than a man, and the time you spent in sleep, for then you are deprived of the use of reason, which only distinguishes man from other creatures, you will find your life to be far shorter than you ever imagined. This time if you compare with the eternity of the world to come, you will find it to be less than a moment. Conjecture, then, the foolish madness of the lovers of this world, who, that they might enjoy one momentary pleasure of this transitory life, do not fear to expose themselves to the loss of eternity.

Then take to your consideration the uncertainty of this life (which is a second misery), for not only is it short, but the brevity itself is most uncertain and doubtful. For who is there that attains to the age of three or four score? How many are extinguished at their very entrance into the world? How many perish in the flower of their youth? You know it not, says Christ, when your Lord is to come, whether in the first watch or second or third or in the cock-crowing. Which, that you may better understand, call to mind especially your domestic friends and other men placed in dignity and authority, whom inexorable death has, at diverse ages (some younger, some older), suddenly taken out of this world, dissipating their vain and long-life promising hopes.

Ponder, fourthly, the inconstancy and mutability of this present life, never continuing in one state. The disposition of the body often changes, not always enjoying health, but subject to frequent diseases; but if you reflect upon the mind, you will see, that, like the troubled ocean, it is tossed up and down with the boisterous winds of her untamed passions, inordinate appetites, and fluctuating cogitations, which upon every occasion do disturb her quiet. Consider, lastly, the instability of the goods of fortune, as they term them, to how many chances they are obnoxious, never suffering the temporal substance to stand still in one stay, thereby to make men happy and prosperous; but, like a wheel, is turned upside down, without any intermission. Consider, also, the continual motion of our life, never resting night nor day, but going forward without ceasing and every day more and more wastes itself; so that it may not unfitly be compared to a candle, which, by little and little, consumes itself, and when it gives the clearest light, the sooner it approaches unto its end; also to a flower, which springs up in the morning, at noon fades and at night wholly withers away.

Which Almighty God, speaking by the Prophet Isaiah of this mutation, excellently reveals in these words: "All flesh is hay, and all the glory of it is like the flower of the field." Which words, St. Jerome expounding, says:

> If one doth rightly consider the frailty of the flesh, and that we grow and decrease according to the moments of hours; never remaining in one state, and that the very thing we now speak, do, or write, passeth away as part of our life, he will not doubt to confess that all flesh is hay, and the glory thereof as a flower, or the green meadows. He that is now an infant will, by and by, be a little child, then presently a young man, growing towards his decrepit age, through uncertain seasons, and before he hath contented himself in youth, feeleth old age to come upon him. The beautiful woman which did draw after her whole troops of gallants in her

youth, her face is now furrowed with deformed wrinkles, and she that before was a pleasure, is now ugly to behold.[1]

Consider fifthly, how deceitful this life is, (which is the worst condition of all, deluding the lovers of this world with a miserable blindness,) for we think it amiable when in itself it is ugly; we think it sweet when it is full of gall and bitterness; when it is circumscribed within the shortest limits, we think it long. When it is full of misery, we think it so happy that there is no danger, no hazard that men will not expose themselves unto, for the conservation of it; yea, with the loss of eternal glory, when they do not fear to commit those sins which make them unworthy of so great felicity.

Consider sixthly, that besides the brevity and other forementioned conditions, that small time wherein we live is subject to innumerable miseries, both spiritual and corporal, that it may well be called a torrent of tears and ocean of infinite molestations. St. Jerome reports how Xerxes, that potent king who overturned mountains and made bridges over the seas, when, from a high place, he beheld that infinite multitude of men and his innumerable army, he wept, to think that not one of those men there present should be alive after a hundred years. And presently adding, "O that we could but ascend into such a turret, to behold the whole earth under our feet, then would I manifest unto you the ruins of the world; nation rising against nation and kingdom against kingdom; some tormented, others slain, some drowned, others led into captivity. Here marrying, here mourning, some born, others dying, some abounding in wealth, others begging. And not only the mighty army of Xerxes, but all the men of the world, in a short space, to be turned to dust and ashes."

Take notice a little of the labors and infirmities of the body, the cogitations and passions of the mind; the diverse dangers in every state and all seasons threatening the ruin of man; and you will every day, more clearly understand the miseries of this life, that when you see what

---

1. Jerome, *Commentary on Isaiah*, Bk. 2, ch. 40.

is to be hoped for in this world, you may with a noble courage contemn it. The last of all these miseries is death, both in respect of soul or body, a thing most terrible, for in this moment the body is disrobed of all things in this world. And the soul in this point receives the joyful or fearful sentence of eternity. These things well considered, you will be instructed how short and miserable the glory of this world is and how it ought to be hated and despised.

A Meditation for Wednesday—On Death

This day you will meditate on death, the consideration of which is very profitable to attain unto true wisdom, to beat down sin and to excite men timely to cast up their accounts, which they are to make in the latter day. Consider, first, the uncertainty of that hour wherein death is to seize upon you, you knowest not the day nor the place nor the state wherein it shall find you; only you believe that you must die, for other things you are wholly ignorant of, except that it sometimes sets upon a man when he little dreams of it and thinks it to be furthest of.

Consider, secondly, that grievous separation which shall be at the point of death, not only from everything of this present life, wherein you look content, but also between the soul and body whose society was most ancient, most loving and dear. If a man takes it grievously to be banished, to be thrust out of his native soil and to be deprived of that air wherein he first breathed, although he should carry all others, his dearest things with him, how far more bitterly would he take that general exile, wherein he most weaned from all worldly things, his house, his means, his father, his mother, his children, his friends, uncertain whither he himself must go. Then, shall he be deprived of the light and the commerce of all human creatures?

If the ox when he is disjoined from his fellow, with whom he was wont in the same yoke to be coupled, with bellowing does express his sorrow, what sobs, what sighs will you fetch, when you will perceive yourself to be violently pulled from these your confederates. Consider, also, that anxiety wherewith the mind of the dying is tormented, when abstracted from all corporal business, he only thinks what shall become of his body and what shall betide his soul, how his body must be cast seven foot into the earth, to be eaten of worms; and what will become of his soul, where it is to remain, he is altogether uncertain; which cogitation does surely much trouble the mind of him that dies when he certainly knows there is heaven or hell to be expected, and he, at equal distance from them both, neither can he tell which of these two contraries will fall to his share.

Another no less affliction follows, that presently he must give a strict account of all his forepassed life to the eternal judge, which men of great sanctity were wont to fear. When Arsenius in the last point of life was seen of his disciples to weep and tremble, they asked him why he feared death, he answered: "Indeed, my children, the fear wherewith ye see me now afflicted, hath quite left me from the time I was first made a monk."[2]

Then all the sins of a man's former life come rushing into his memory, representing themselves unto him, as it were in battle array, to destroy him, but especially his grievous sins wherein he took greatest delight are continually present to his fancy, which do so torment him that they drive him into a dangerous despair of his salvation, and the remembrance of those pleasures, which before were grateful, are now most bitter unto him. That the wise man saith true: "Look not upon the wine when it is yellow, when the color thereof shineth in the glass: it goeth in pleasantly, but in the end, it will bite like a snake, and will spread abroad poison like a basilisk" (Prov 23:31–32).

Such a poisoned cup the enemy of mankind presents to the lovers of the world to drink. Such is the liquor of the outward gilded cup of Babylon. Wicked man, seeing himself environed with so many accusers, begins then to fear the success of his latter judgment, and to bewail himself with bitter outcries, "O miserable and unhappy man that have

---

2. Simon Metaphrastes, in his *Lives*, vol. 4, according to Sarium.

lived thus long in darkness, and walked in the footsteps of iniquity, what shall now become of me? If St. Paul saith, 'such as a man soweth, such he shall reap' (Gal 6:8), I that have sowed nothing else but the works of the flesh, what should I expect but corruption?"

If St. John says that no unclean thing shall enter into that heavenly city, which is paved with burnished gold, what part shall I have therein, that am defiled with all kind of luxury? Then follow the sacraments of the Church: Confession, Communion, Extreme Unction, which are the last helps of our holy mother the Catholic Church, to succour his dying soul. From all these aforesaid circumstances, you may gather with what anxiety a wicked man is oppressed at the hour of his departure. Then he will wish that he had led a better life, and what great austerity he would use if longer time might be permitted to him. Then would he vehemently implore the divine assistance, but the greatness of his infirmity and the pangs of death approaching, will not suffer him, which will be so great that he shall scarce be able to turn his thoughts upon God. Behold, after these, the symptoms of this last infirmity, forerunners of death and harbingers of your last end, which certainly in themselves are horrible and to the beholders terrible. The stomach swells, the speech fails, the feet begin to die, the knees wax cold, the nostrils fall, the eyes sink, the face waxes pale, the tongue can no longer perform its office; finally, the striving of the soul going out of the body disturbs all the senses and leaves them wholly without vigor.

But who is able to express the anguish of the soul which is far greater? For then it is in a mighty agony, both in regard of the doubtful event of her salvation, and of the strict account she is presently to make of the deeds of her whole life; as also, because she naturally loves the body, she cannot be separated from it but with great affliction, especially, knowing not what shall become of her. Having well contemplated the soul departing the body, you must yet make two journeys more: one in accompanying the body to the grave, the other in following the soul to the deciding of her cause. And you will see the event of both. Mark, therefore, the dead carcass how they prepare a winding sheet for it. What expedition they use to carry it out of the house. Consider the solemnity and rites wherewith it is carried to the grave. How the bells ring, and everyone inquire of the dead. The office of the Church also, the prayers of the standers by, the doleful tune of the Church, while the body is carried to the grave and buried. The tears of friends and kindred, and all those ceremonies which are wont to be performed about the dead.

Leaving the body under the earth, accompany the soul passing to a new and unknown region, where she expects the sentence of the eternal judge. Imagine with yourself that you are present at this tribunal, and the whole court of heaven, waiting with deep silence and great attention the event and sentence of this judgment, here must be given a strict account of all receivings and disbursements. I say account, of your life, of your goods, of your family, of the divine inspirations, of the means and occasions to live well, and finally of the Blood of Jesus Christ, and the use of his sacraments, and according as his account is, so the sentence shall be pronounced.

A Meditation for Thursday—On the Last Judgment

This day you will meditate upon the last judgment, to the end that you may stir up in your soul two principal effects which every Christian soul ought to have, to wit, the fear of God and hatred of sin. Place, therefore, first before thine eyes, how terrible that day will be wherein all the litigious causes of the sons of Adam shall be decided and a final end put to the processes of our whole life, and what shall be ordained of those for all eternity shall be publicly pronounced to the view of the whole world. This day comprehends in it all the days of all ages, past, present, and to come, and exacts a severe account of all the actions of all men, pouring out all the fury upon men, heaped up together from forepassed ages; because then the torrent of Almighty God's vengeance shall overflow beyond its limits, rushing with a greater violence, by how much more it was the longer detained and at once shall overwhelm all iniquity from the creation of the world. Consider, secondly, the dreadful signs which shall go before this day. For our Savior says: "And there shall be signs in the sun, and in the moon, and in the stars" (Lk 21:25).

And all creatures of heaven and earth shall tremble, understanding their ruin to be at hand. Men also, as our Savior says, worn and withered away, perceiving the horrible raging of the sea; and they themselves scarce a hair's breadth distant from death. Seeing also the mighty risings and inundations of the water; and by these conjecturing the calamities and misery these prodigious signs threaten to the world, will be amazed with such a horror that they will be without life, without voice, without colour or human shape; they will be dead before they die, dreading their damnation before the sentence be pronounced, imagining the future pain by their present distemper. Then everyone out of exceeding fear will be so solicitous of himself that he will nothing regard others whosoever they be, parents, or husbands, or wives, or friends, or companions.

Imagine, thirdly, the universal deluge of fire which shall go before this judgment; that dreadful noise of the trumpet which one of the archangels shall blow, wherewith all the people of the whole world shall be summoned together in one place, making their appearance before the judgment seat; and last of all, that dreadful majesty, the supreme Judge of the quick and dead, shall assume to himself upon this tribunal. Fourthly, consider what exact account shall be required of everyone. Holy Job says: "Indeed, I know it is so, and that man cannot be justified, compared with God. If he will contend with him, he cannot answer him one for a thousand" (Job 9:2–3).

What then shall become of man when God shall begin to handle him according to the rigor of his justice, when he shall speak to his conscience inwardly? O wicked and perverse man, what have you seen in me, that out of the height of impiety, despising me, you should join with my enemies? I have created you according to mine own image and likeness; I have illuminated you with the light of faith; I have seasoned you in the Christian faith from your infancy; I have redeemed you with my own blood; for your sake I have fasted, watched, prayed, undergone tedious journeys, sweat blood, and endured many more miseries in the course of my life; for the love of you, I have suffered persecutions, injuries, blasphemies, and the very Cross itself. This Cross is my witness, these nails my witnesses, which you seest imprinted in my hands and feet; to conclude, heaven and earth that did behold my Passion are my witnesses. How I have drawn your soul. How I have redeemed you with the ransom of my precious blood.

How have you esteemed this precious pearl bought by me with an inestimable price? O generation of vipers, why have you chosen to serve my enemy with a great deal of pain and neglected your duty towards me, your Creator and Redeemer, which you mightest have performed with a great deal of pleasure? I have called you and you would not answer to my vocation. I have knocked at the door of your heart and you have refused me entrance. I have stretched my arms upon the Cross and you have not regarded me; you despise my counsels, promises, and threatenings. Pronounce, therefore, ye angels, the sentence, and be judges between me and my vineyard. "What is there that I ought to do more to my vineyard, that I have not done to it?" (Is 5:4).

What will the reprobate and scoffers at divine mysteries answer? They that have hissed at virtue, derided simplicity, and observed better the laws of the world than of God; they that have stopped their ears at the voice of God; they who have contemned his divine inspirations; they who have been rebellious against his commandments and ungrateful for his benefits. What will those libertines say, who letting themselves loose to all vices, have lived as if there were no God at all or that he did not regard the things that are done below? What will those say, who have followed their commodities, lust, and pleasure for a law? "What will you do in the day of visitation, and of the calamity which cometh from afar? to whom will ye flee for help? and where will ye leave your glory? That you be not bowed down under the bond, and fall with the slain?" (Is 10:3–4).

Fifthly, consider that terrible sentence which, after judgment, the supreme Judge pronounces against the wicked; which he will thunder out with such a dreadful noise, that at the sound thereof, the ears of the standers-by will ring, as the prophet Isaias says: "His lips are filled with indignation, and his tongue as a devouring fire" (Is 30:27). For what flames can be so ardent as those words: "Depart from me, you cursed, into everlasting fire which was prepared for the devil and his angels" (Mt 25:41). Every word of which sentence is full of bitter torment. For who is able to comprehend what this separation is, what curse, what fire, what society, and, finally, what eternity, to which the wicked are adjudged by force of this sentence?

A Meditation for Friday—On The Pains of Hell

This day you will meditate upon the torments of hell, that duly pondering them you may have more awe of Almighty God and a greater hatred of sin. St. Bonaventure teaches that "these torments are to be considered according to certain similitudes set down by holy men, concerning this matter. Wherefore, it will not be beside our purpose (as the same Doctor, in the same place saith,) to imagine hell a horrible confused chaos, a lake under the earth, a deep fiery dungeon; or as a spacious city, dark and terrible, burning with obscure and fearful fire, filled with wailings, howlings, weeping, for the inexplicable pains. In this miserable and unhappy place, are two kinds of torments, the punishment of sense, and the punishment of loss of Almighty God."[3]

Consider that there is no outward or inward sense of the damned which is not afflicted with a proper torment; for as the damned, in all their members and senses, have offended God, using them as instruments and weapons whereby, neglecting the society and law of God, they served sin, so the divine justice has ordained that every sense,

---

3. *The Soliloquies of St. Bonaventure*, "A Bundle of Myrrh from the Passion of Christ," ch. 3.

according to their desert, should be tormented with a proper punishment; the wanton and lascivious eyes shall be tortured with the hideous aspect of devils. The ears which were open to lies, detractions, and other impurities, shall ring with unwonted clamours, outcries, and blasphemies. The noses which were delighted with sweet odours shall be poisoned with an intolerable stink. The taste which was glutted with dainty fare shall be tormented with intolerable hunger and thirst. The tongue which uttered detractions and murmurings shall drink the gall of dragons. The wanton, which gave consent to their brutish desires, shall be frozen with extreme cold, and as holy Job saith: "Let him pass from the snow waters to excessive heat" (24:19).

The interior senses also shall not want their torments: the imagination shall be tormented with the apprehension of present pains, the memory with the calling to mind of forepast pleasures, the understanding with the fear of future griefs, the will with an incredible hatred and raging towards God.

There, as St. Gregory saith, shall be intolerable cold, unquenchable fire, a never dying worm, a stench which none is able to endure, horrid darkness, grievous whippings, visages of devils, confusion of sinners, and desperation of all good. Tell me, I pray you, could you endure one little moment the least part of these torments? Surely it would be very grievous if not intolerable for you. What then will it be to suffer this whole inundation of evils at one time in all your members and senses, external and internal, not one or a thousand nights, but for all eternity? What sense, what tongue, what mind of man is able to conceive or express these things? Neither are these the greatest torments the damned suffer. There remains yet a more grievous, which the divines do call the punishment of loss, which consists in the perpetual privation of the beatifical vision of God and his saints and of all that glorious and blessed society. For that is the greatest torment that deprives man of the most excellent good. Seeing, therefore, that God is that effectual and chief good of all goods, to be deprived of him must needs be the greatest of all evils. These are the general torments of the damned; besides these, there are other particular torments, wherewith everyone according to their sins are afflicted. The proud, the envious, the covetous, the luxurious, and other vicious have their peculiar torments; the measure of pain there shall be proportional to their glory and pleasure here; poverty and want to plenty, hunger and thirst to gluttony and to former delights.

To all these aforesaid torments, eternity is yet to be added, which is, as it were, the seal and key of all the rest; for if at length they should have an end, they were some way tolerable. That which is restrained to a certain time cannot be so insufferable; but this punishment is everlasting, without solace, without relaxation, without diminution, where remains no hope of an end of their torments, or tormentors, or themselves that suffer them, but is, as it were, a perpetual and irrevocable banishment, never to be recalled, which is a thing of importance to be noted, that the mind may be stirred up, thereby, to that saving fear and love of God. From the eternity of torments proceeds that great hatred wherewith they are incensed against God. Hence proceed these horrible blasphemies and curses, which with their impure mouths they rail at God, saying, "cursed be God who has created us, and has condemned us to an everlasting death, which does so oppress and torment us, that notwithstanding never kills. Cursed be his power, which does so grievously afflict us. Cursed be his wisdom, that has laid open all our wickedness. Cursed be his justice, that has exacted eternal punishment for temporal sins. Cursed be his Cross, which has not benefited us. Cursed be his blood, that was shed, seeing it requires revenge against us. Cursed be the Mother of God, who although she be pious and propitious to all, yet notwithstanding has showed herself to us cruel and unmerciful. Cursed be all the saints of God reigning with Christ, and rejoicing at our miseries." These are the hymns, this is that harsh melody which the damned do continually jar, railing at the Almighty God with detested blasphemies for all eternity.

A Meditation for Saturday—On Heaven

This day you will meditate upon the glory of the saints of God, which may more eagerly inflame your soul to contemn the vanities of this world, and aspire to that eternal felicity. To the end that you may get a better knowledge and gust of this inestimable glory, consider these five things. First, the excellency of the place. Secondly, the joy of that society. Thirdly, the vision of God. Fourthly, the glory of their bodies. Fifthly, the complete perfection of all abundant good. In the excellency of the place, take notice of the admirable and wonderful spaciousness of it; in approved authors you readest that the least of the fixed stars of heaven is bigger than the whole earth, and some of them do exceed the earth two or three hundred times in bigness. Then cast up thine eyes to heaven and consider the innumerable multitude of them in the firmament and you will see a great deal of void space where many more may be placed. How can you then but be astonished at the greatness of so rare a fabric? Then consider the beauty of that place which no tongue is able to express, for if Almighty God, in this place of banishment and vale of misery, has made many things of admirable and comely hue, of what great beauty, and how much adorned do you think that place to be which God would have to be the ordinary seat of his glory, the palace of his majesty, the mansion of the elect and the paradise of all pleasure?

After the beauty of the place, consider the nobility of the inhabitants, whose number, sanctity, riches, and glory are far beyond our imagination. St. John said, the multitude are so great that they are innumerable. St. Dionysius affirms that the multitude of angels do far exceed the number of sublunary creatures. Whom St. Thomas following, thinks, that as the heavens by many degrees exceed the bigness of the earth, being but, as it were, a point of them; so proportionably the glorious spirits therein contained, do surpass all earthly things. What can be thought more admirable? Assuredly this well pondered would make a man lose himself in the abyss of Almighty God's goodness.

Yes, without comparison every one of these blessed spirits is far more beautiful to the eye than all this visible world. Oh, what would it be to contemplate the incomprehensible number of so rare and glorious spirits, and to understand their several offices and perfections? How the angels bring messages; how the archangels minister; how the principalities triumph; how the powers rejoice; how the dominations bear sway; how the virtues shine; how the thrones do glitter; how the cherubim do illuminate; how the seraphim do burn with love; and, finally, how all with one unanimous consent do praise Almighty God. If the conversation and fellowship of good men be so delightful, what pleasure will it be to be associated with so great a multitude of saints? "To be conversant with the Apostles, to talk with the prophets, to discourse with martyrs, and to enjoy the blessed familiarity of all the elect? Oh, but what will it be to enjoy his presence whom the morning stars do magnify?" whose beauty the sun and moon admire; before whom the holy angels and all the celestial spirits do prostrate themselves. That *summum bonum*, that infinite good, which in itself comprehends all good whatsoever; oh, what content will the heart of man feel, to behold him, who is one and all, who although he be most simple without composition, yet contains in himself the perfections of all things created? What can the heart of man desire greater?

If it were so much to see and hear king Solomon, that the queen of Sheba coming from far remote parts, moved with his great wisdom, should say, "Blessed are thy men, and blessed are thy servants, who stand before thee always and hear thy wisdom" (1 Kings 10:8). What would it be to behold that true Solomon, that eternal wisdom, that immense majesty, that inestimable beauty, that infinite goodness? And, which is more, to enjoy him for all eternity? This is the essential and truest glory of the saints; this is the last end and centre of all our wishes. Consider, moreover, the glory of their bodies which shall be beautified with these four gifts: subtility, agility, impassibility and clarity; which will be so great, that every one of the elect, as our Blessed Savior saith, shall glitter like the sun in the kingdom of his Father. If one only sun does so rejoice and illuminate this universe, what do you think so many brighter suns will do which shall there shine?

What should I speak of other joys which there shall be? Health without infirmity, liberty without violence, beauty without deformity, immortality without corruption, abundance without want, rest without trouble, security without fear, riches without poverty, joy without sorrow, honor without contradiction. There, as St. Augustine says[4] shall be true glory, when everyone shall be commended without error or flattery. True honor shall be denied to none that is worthy of it, and it shall be given to none unworthy, neither shall any unworthy attempt it there, where none shall be permitted but the worthy. There shall be true peace, where they shall suffer no contradiction from themselves or others; the reward of virtue shall be he which gave virtue. And he has promised to give himself, that which nothing can be better, or greater than. For what other thing is it, that he spoke by the prophet: "I will be their God, and they shall be my people" (Ezek 37:27). If I do not, who is it that can satiate their souls? I will be that good which can possibly be desired of man, their life, their peace, their honor. For so is that understood which the Apostle speaketh: "that God be in all." He shall be the end of all our desires, which shall be contemplated without end, shall be loved without tediousness, shall be praised without ceasing.

The place of the saints, if you do behold the spaciousness of it, it shall be most ample, if the beauty, most delicious; if the splendour, most exceedingly bright. There shall be admirable delightful society, no vicissitude of times, the day shall not succeed the night, nor the night the day, but all time shall be there alike. There shall be one perpetual spring, which the Holy Ghost, with a wonderful temper, shall always make green and flourishing; there shall all celebrate everlasting holidays, rejoicing with unspeakable gladness; there shall all sound their instruments of music and sing praises to him, by whose power they live and

___
4. Augustine, *The City of God*, Bk. 22, ch. 30.

reign for all eternity. O celestial city, secure habitation, palace flowing with all delights, people without murmuring, quiet citizens, men without poverty. Oh, that I may at length enjoy thee. Oh, that the days of my banishment were ended. When will that joyful day come? When shall I go out of this mortality? When shall I come and appear before thy face, O God?

A Meditation for Sunday—On the Benefits of God

This day you will spend in reflecting on Almighty God's benefits, that you may be grateful to him for the same, and your heart inflamed with the love of him, that has heaped so many favors upon you; which seeing they be innumerable, you will take four of the chief to your consideration, which are the benefits of your creation, preservation, redemption, and vocation, besides particular benefits specially bestowed upon you.

Touching the benefit of your creation, examine diligently what you were before, what God has given you when you had no precedent merits. Behold your comely body well composed of its members and senses; look upon your noble soul, beautified with these excellent faculties, the understanding, will, and memory. Remember, that when he gave you your soul, he gave you all things, seeing there is no perfection in any creature, which is not found more excellent in the soul of man. Hence it manifestly follows that when God bestowed this great benefit upon you, he with it bestowed what else soever you have. Concerning the benefit of your conservation and preservation, consider that all your being depends upon the divine providence and disposure, without which you cannot move a foot or subsist the least moment of time. Moreover, for your use he has created the whole universal world and all things therein contained: the earth, the sea, birds, fishes, beasts, plants, the very angels themselves he has ordained to do you service. Consider your health, the strength of limbs and your very life itself, which you enjoy, to be the great benefits of Almighty God, who, by daily nourishment and other temporal helps, conserves all these in their proper vigor. Observe the miseries and tribulations unto which other mortal men are subject, into which, as others, you had easily fallen, had not the divine goodness protected you.

In the benefit of your redemption, consider the abundant good, both in quantity and quality, which he has purchased to you by it. Then call to mind the bitterness of his torments, which he suffered in soul and body to ease you; and that the acknowledgment of these favors may take a greater impression in you, in the mystery of his Passion take notice of these four things. First, who is it that suffers; secondly, what he suffered; thirdly, for whom he suffered; fourthly, why he suffered. He that suffered was God; what he suffered were the most grievous torments, and such that never any mortal man did endure the like. For whom? For most ungrateful creatures, cursed and worthy of hell fire. Why? Not for any commodity or profit of his own or that we had merited so much by our precedent merits, but only moved to it by his infinite love and bounty towards us. Concerning the benefit of your vocation, consider the grace he gave you when he infused into you the Christian faith by the receiving of Baptism and other sacraments, when he did enroll you in the book of his eternity amongst faithful souls. If, after your first vocation, when by sin you had lost the innocence of Baptism, he has drawn you again out of the mire of your own corruption, restored you to grace, and brought you back again into the way of your own salvation.

What thanksgiving ought you to render unto him for so great a benefit? How great was his mercy to you, that with longanimity he expected so many years; that he permitted you to spend your days in so great impurity of wickedness; that he has often visited you with good and holy inspirations; that he did not cut off the thread of your perverse life as he served others in the same place; to conclude, that he called you with such efficacious grace that he restored you from death to life and opened thine eyes to contemplate his clear light. How great was his clemency towards you that he supported you with his grace, not to return back again to your former sins, but to overcome the enemies of mankind and constantly to persevere in a virtuous cause. These are the common benefits. Besides these, there are many secret ones known to none but those that receive them, and others which, indeed, are not clearly known unto themselves, but only to him that bestowed them. How often for your pride, arrogance, ingratitude, and sloth have you deserved to be left of God, as many for less causes have been? Yet, notwithstanding, he would not? How often has God, with his singular providence, exempted you from evil, removed occasions of offending, broken the snare that the enemy had laid for your perdition, has frustrated his expectation and would not permit that his counsels and machinations should prevail against you? How often has he done to us as he did to St. Peter in the gospel: "Behold Satan hath desired to have you, that he may sift you as wheat: But I have prayed for thee, that thy faith fail not" (Lk 22:31–32).

And who can know these secret benefits but God alone? Benefits which are palpable are easy to be seen, but those which are private, consisting in the working of good or preventing of ill, the mind of man cannot perfectly comprehend. Wherefore, it is meet and convenient to reason that we should render immortal thanks to God for all these benefits and confess ingenuously that we have received more than we are able to restore, and that our obligations towards him are so great that with any goods of ours we shall never live to requite them, when we cannot so much as number or comprehend them in our understanding.

Of the Time and Fruit of These Meditations

Behold, Christian reader, you have seven former meditations, accommodated to every day of the week; not so that it is an offence to meditate upon another matter when, as we said before, whatsoever inflames the heart to the love and fear of God and to the keeping of his commandments may profitably be assumed for matter of meditation. We, therefore, out of so great a number have selected these, both for that they contain the chief mysteries of our faith and that in them is force and efficacy to rouse up our souls to the love and fear of God; as also to set before novices which have need of a guide, prepared and, as it were, ruminate on the matter, lest they confusedly wander up and down in this spacious field without any certainty, now meditating upon one thing and presently on another.

The former meditations to whom they properly belong: Moreover, these meditations, as we have said elsewhere, suit best with those who do begin to turn to Almighty God from their wicked courses. For these had need to be helped by consideration of these things, to the detestation and horror of sin, the fear of God, the contempt of the world, which are, as it were, the first steps to the amendment of our former perverse life; therefore, it is good that they should sometimes insist in them, that they may have the better foundation for other ensuing virtues.

SEVEN OTHER MEDITATIONS ON THE PASSION OF OUR LORD

Here follow seven other meditations of the Passion of Christ, his Resurrection and Ascension into heaven; to which, others of his holy life may well be added. But we must note that in the Passion of our Blessed Savior, six things chiefly are to be meditated upon. First, the bitterness of his sorrow, that we may empathetically suffer with him. Secondly, the greatness of our sins, which were the cause of his torments, that we may abhor them. Thirdly, the greatness of the benefit, that we may be grateful for it. Fourthly, the excellency of the divine charity and bounty therein manifested, that we may love him more fervently. Fifthly, the convenience of the mystery, that we may be drawn to admiration of it. Lastly, the multiplicity of virtues of our Blessed Savior which did shine in this stupendous mystery, that we may partly imitate and partly admire them; wherefore, in the midst of these meditations, let us sometimes enter in to the sufferings with our Blessed Savior in the extremity of his sorrows; extreme indeed, both by reason of the tenderness of his body, as also, for the great affection he bore unto our souls.

He did suffer them without any manner of consolation, as we shall speak hereafter in its proper place. Sometimes, let us stir up in ourselves compunction for our sins, which were the cause of these his great sufferings. Sometimes, let us kindle in our souls an ardent affection, considering his great affection towards us, which upon the Cross he declared and manifested to the whole world. And the benefit which he bestowed upon us in his Passion, because he bought us with the inestimable price of his precious blood, of which only we reap the benefit and commodity. Sometimes, let us ruminate upon the convenience of the manner his eternal wisdom would be pleased to choose to cure our miseries, to satisfy for our sins, to relieve our necessities, to make us partakers of his glory, to repress our pride, to induce us to the love and joyful suffering of poverty, injuries, austerity, and all commendable laborious exercises. Moreover, it will not be besides the matter to look into the admirable examples which did principally shine in the life and Passion of our sweet Savior, his meekness, patience, obedience, mercy, poverty, charity, humility, bounty, modesty, and other of his rare virtues, which in all his actions did glitter like stars in the firmament. And chiefly to this end, let us meditate upon these things, that, as near as we can, we may imitate them. Let us shake off sloth and elevate our souls, that as much as in our power lies, with the help of his holy grace, we may trace his sacred footsteps. This is the best and most profitable method of meditating upon our Blessed Savior's Passion, that is to say, that thereby we be drawn to imitation and so to be wholly transformed into our Blessed Savior, that each one may say with the Apostle: "And I live, now not I; but Christ liveth in me" (Gal 2:20).

Moreover, in meditating on our Blessed Savior's Passion, we must set him before the eyes of our souls, imagining that we see as present the pangs of his heavy sufferings; and we must not only insist upon the bare history of his Passion, but we must consider other circumstances; namely, these four: First, who it is that suffers? Secondly, for whom? Thirdly, how? Fourthly, why?

First, he that suffers is God, omnipotent, infinite, immense. For whom? The most ungrateful creature in the world and less regarding his benefits. How? With most profound humility, charity, bounty, meekness, mercy, patience, modesty, etc. Why? Not for his own commodity, nor our merits, but for his immense piety, mercy, goodness, and love towards us.

Last of all, let us not only contemplate his outward, but his inward torments, for much more may be considered in the soul than in the body of Christ, both for the more sensible feeling of his Passion there, as also for diverse other considerations therein. Thus, having set down this short preface, let us proceed to the handling of the mysteries themselves of our Blessed Savior's Passion.

A Meditation for Monday—On the Washing of the Feet and the Institution of the Blessed Sacrament

This day, after you have signed yourself with the Sign of the Cross, you will meditate upon the washing of the disciples' feet and institution of the Blessed Sacrament.

Consider, O my soul, at this supper, sweet Jesus himself to be present; contemplate that inestimable example of humility which he there proposed unto you for imitation, when rising from the table where he sat with his disciples, he would be pleased to wash their feet. O sweet Jesus, what is it that you do? O sweet Jesus, why does your mighty Majesty thus diminish itself? O my soul, what would you have thought to see God kneeling at the feet of men and prostrate before Judas? O barbarous and cruel man, could not so great humility mollify your heart? Was not so great bounty and sweetness able to penetrate your entrails and to reclaim you from your intended mischief? Can it be that you determined to sell this meek lamb for so small a price? Nay, if it be so, how could you yet endure to behold so rare an example? I wonder, did it not wound your guilty soul with compunction for your grievous crime? O delicate hands, how could you touch so filthy, sordid, and sin-contaminated feet? O pure and unspotted hands, how could you endure to wash those feet that were stained with going and coming to make a sale of your precious blood?

O thrice happy Apostles, did you not tremble and stand amazed at the sight of so great humility? What do you do, Peter? Can you permit the Lord of Majesty to wash your feet? St. Peter, wholly astonished with the admiration of this spectacle, when he saw our Blessed Savior falling down at his feet, cried out, "Lord, dost thou wash my feet?" What, are not you the Son of the ever-living God? Are not you the Creator of the whole world, the beauty of heaven, the paradise of angels, redeemer of mankind, splendour of your Father's glory, most deep fountain of the eternal wisdom? And do you wash my feet? How does it come to pass, that you Lord of so great majesty and glory, should thus debase yourself to so vile a service?

Then, consider how he washed all his disciples' feet, one by one, and after washing, wiped them with a linen cloth wherewith he was girded. Open the eyes of your mind to behold in these mysteries a representation of our redemption. This linen cloth so wiped their feet that all the dirt which was upon their feet did stick on the linen cloth, not without mystery. For what more foul than man conceived in sin? What more pure than Christ conceived by the operation of the Holy Spirit? "My beloved," saith the spouse in the canticles "is white, and ruddy chosen out of thousands" (Song 5:10); yet, notwithstanding, most pure, most beautiful. Christ took unto himself all the spots of our souls; from which, that he might cleanse us, (as you may see him upon the Cross), he would be pleased to defile himself with the filth of our impurity. Consider, lastly, with what words our Blessed Savior closed up this humble action: "For I have given you an example, that as I have done to you, so you do also" (Jn 13:15). Which words do not only pertain to this present action and example of humility, but likewise to all the actions of Christ throughout his whole life, which is a most absolute and perfect rule for us to square our actions by, especially of humility, which is here to life represented unto us.

Of The Institution Of The Blessed Sacrament

The causes why Christ instituted this Sacrament: He that desires to comprehend anything of this noble mystery must certainly think that no tongue is able to express that immense love and ardent affection, wherewith our Blessed Savior was inflamed towards his holy Church and all faithful souls, in instituting this stupendous mystery.

The First: For when Christ the bridegroom determined to depart out of this mortal life and to leave the Church his beloved spouse, lest this departure should be any occasion to her of forgetting her redeemer, he gave her this Sacrament wherein he himself is present as a pledge and memorial of his perpetual love.

The Second: Then seeing he was to be long absent, lest his spouse should remain solitary alone, he, for his consolation, would leave himself for her companion in this holy Sacrament.

The Third: When our Blessed Savior was to suffer death for the redemption of his spouse, to enrich her with his most Precious Blood, and to purge her from sins, lest she should be defrauded of so great a treasure; he would give her a key in this Sacrament whereby she might at her pleasure enjoy these riches; for as St. Chrysostom saith, we must think as often as we come to this Sacrament, we put our mouth to the bleeding side of Christ and from thence drink his most Precious Blood, whose merits we participate.

The Fourth: Moreover, this celestial bridegroom did desire to be tenderly beloved of his spouse, and for this cause would leave her this mystical food, consecrated with most efficacious words, and therein so great virtue, that whosoever receives it worthily shall presently be struck with the darts of love.

The Fifth: He would likewise bestow upon his spouse some pure pledge, thereby to make her secure of the certain succession of future glory, that in hope of so great a good, he might temper the laborious difficulty and make the tedious bitterness of this present life to be more tolerable; wherefore, that the spouse might certainly believe that she shall at length attain to these unspeakable goods, he has given her for a pawn this inestimable treasure, which is as much worth as that which is expected hereafter; that she should not doubt but that God will give her himself in glory, where he lives in spirit, that would be pleased to give her himself in this vale of tears, where he lives in the flesh.

The Sixth: He would, moreover, when he died, make his last will and testament, wherein he left to his spouse a singular manna to cure all her infirmities; a gift than which nothing can be more sovereign, nothing more precious, seeing the Deity itself is therein contained.

The Seventh: Lastly, he desired to feed our souls with some heavenly food, seeing they need no less nourishment that they might live spiritually than the body needs corporal sustenance, that she might live corporally. Wherefore, this spiritual physician, when he had diligently examined and felt the pulse of our fragility, instituted this holy Sacrament which he exhibited unto us under the species or form of bread, that he might declare what effect it should work in us, that is to say, that it is as necessary for our souls as bread for the body.

A Meditation for Tuesday—On the Prayer in the Garden, the Arrest, and the Events Before Annas

This day you will meditate on the prayer Christ made in the garden, the method thereof, and the offenses he suffered in the house of Annas. Consider, therefore, how Christ our Lord, after the consummation of his mystical body with his disciples, before he entered into the tragedy of his Passion, went to make his prayer upon the mount Olivet; whereby he would instruct us, that in all adversities and tribulations of this present life, we fly to prayer as to a holy anchor; the power of which is so great that it either beats back the forces of tribulations, or (which is of greater excellency) ministers sufficient strength to endure them with a constant and willing mind.

He took, for his companions in his journey, three of his disciples whom he loved above the rest: St. Peter, St. James, and St. John. Who, as they were eyewitnesses of his transfiguration, so likewise, they should be present in his agony to behold him, for the love of man, now transformed into a far more different shape than he was when he manifested himself unto them in a glorious and glittering form. That, also, he might open unto them his inward grief to be much greater than appeared outwardly. He saith unto them: "My soul is sorrowful even unto death: stay you here, and watch with me" (Mt 26:38). O words full of compassion! Then departing from his disciples a stone's cast, with great submission and reverence, he prayed his Father: "My Father, if it be possible, let this chalice pass from me. Nevertheless, not as I will, but as thou wilt." Which prayer, when he had repeated thrice, he fell into such an agony that he sweat drops of blood, trickling down upon the earth from his precious body. Consider that partly the foreseeing of the most unspeakable torments that ever any mortal man suffered, prepared for his most tender body; partly the distinct representation of the sins of the whole world for the expiation of which he was now to suffer death upon the Cross; partly the remembrance of the ingratitude of many who would not esteem or reap any profit from this great benefit, struck such a deep impression into his soul, that it filled it with sad and incredible anxiety, so troubled his senses and tender flesh that all the elements of his body being weakened, the opened pores on every side sweat out drops of blood.

If the flesh, which properly suffered not this anguish, but only through a simple imagination, was thus afflicted, what did his soul feel? To whom, properly, these sorrows did appertain. His prayer being ended, that counterfeit friend of Christ, Judas the traitor, came attended with a hellish band. He, I say, who renounced his apostleship, to be head and captain of a troop of hellhounds, behold in the forefront of that wicked multitude, impudently coming to his Master, whom before he had sold, betraying him with a kiss of peace and friendship. In that hour, said Jesus to the company which came to apprehend him, "Are ye come out, as it were against a thief, with swords and clubs? When I was daily with you in the temple, you did not stretch forth your hands against me: but this is your hour, and the power of darkness" (Lk 22:52–53).

This mystery is worthy of admiration, for what thing can be more admirable and stupendous, than to see the only begotten Son of God, not only in the form of sinful man, but in the shape of a condemned man: "This is your hour, and the power of darkness." From which words is gathered that this innocent lamb was left to the diabolical cruelty of the princes of darkness, who, by their minions and ministers, poured all the malice and mischief they were able to conceive against him. Consider how much, for your sake, the supreme majesty of God is humbled; to endure all the extremity of torments that ever any suffered in this present life, not to die for his own faults, but for your sins; but he did undergo this of his own accord, to free you from the power of Satan. He had scarce spoken these words when that whole rabble of hunger-starved wolves, gaping after their prey, rushed upon this meek and innocent lamb, hauling, tearing, and afflicting him, with as much cruelty as ever they could. O barbarous and inhuman proceedings! O cruel and savage blows, contumelious violences, wherewith they tormented him; they insulted after a horrid manner, no otherwise than conquerors return loaded with spoils, after they have put to flight their enemies, or hunters when they have caught their prey. The hands which a little before were exercised in working miracles were now bound with ropes so cruelly that they razed the skin and besmeared them with blood. Thus they led him through the public streets of Jerusalem, following him with contumelies and blows. Behold him in this journey going alone, left by all his disciples, compassed with a multitude of his enemies, forced to make such haste that he was wholly out of breath, his color changed, his face blushing, and his whole body weakened and wearied by reason of the intolerable present difficulty.

Although our Blessed Savior was barbarously and almost cruelly handled by that blood-sucking multitude, yet, nevertheless, you might have seen in his countenance a pleasant sweetness, in his eyes a comely gravity, in his manners a divine grace, which all the torments of the whole world could not so much as diminish in the least degree. After this, go with our Blessed Savior into the house of Annas the high priest, that there you may take notice what favor he reaped for his mild answer, when Annas examined him of his and his disciples' doctrine, which was that one of the officers gave him a cruel blow upon his cheek, saying, "Answerest thou the high priest so?" To him Christ replied: "If I have spoken evil, give testimony of the evil; but if well, why strikest thou me?" (Jn 18:23). Behold, O my soul, not only the mild answer, but the print of the officer's hand in his tender cheek, his countenance, notwithstanding, quiet and amiable, not a whit moved at the shame of so great an affront, because he inwardly thought so low and humbly of himself that he had turned the other side without delay, if the rascal had desired it.

A Meditation for Wednesday—On the Events Before Caiphas, the Denial of St. Peter, and the Scourging

This day you will consider how Christ our Lord was offered up to Caiphas the high priest; what torments he endured there all that night; how St. Peter denied him; and last of all, how cruelly he was scourged. Consider, first of all, how he was led from the house of Annas to the house of Caiphas; it is worth your pains to follow him thither; for there you will see the mighty sun of justice eclipsed; there you will behold that divine face upon which the angels themselves delight to gaze, deformed with the filthy spittings of the Jews; for our Blessed Savior standing in the midst of them was conjured by the high priest in the name of his Father to speak out what he was. He answered appropriately; but they, who were unworthy of such an answer, blinded with the splendour of this great light like mad dogs, rushed upon him, vomiting up the bitter gall of their whole malice against him.

They began, whole troops of them to buffet him, to beat and kick him, they spat upon his divine face and threw the very filth of their noses upon it. Others hoodwinked his eyes with a dirty linen cloth, smiting him upon his cheek and would in mockery have him prophecy who it was that struck him. O admirable and unheard-of patience and humility of the only begotten Son of God. Oh, behold that face, which the angels of heaven do contemplate with incredible joy, besmeared with their sordid and filthy spittings. Men, when they spit, commonly turn themselves to some foul place, somewhat remote from the sight of others. In this palace was there no place found more contemptible therein to cast their spit and filthy drivel than the sacred face of Jesus Christ? O man that are but dust and ashes, can you choose but be stirred up to humility and contempt of yourself at so rare an example? Consider, moreover, what torments our Blessed Savior suffered all that night, how the officers that kept him afflicted him, that sleep should not close his eyes, derided the supreme Majesty of God and loaded him with many injurious sufferings.

Weigh with yourself, my soul, that now your spouse is made the white and mark, receiving upon himself all the darts of injurious crosses that the mischievous Jews could shoot at him. O cruel night, O unquiet night, in which you Blessed Jesus could rest no more by reason of anguish and affliction, than others who took pleasure to torment you. The night was ordained for the rest of all creatures, that the members and senses wearied with the labor of the day before might then take some repose. But the wicked soldiers that kept you spent it in tormenting your senses, they did bind your body, troubled your soul, fettered your hands and feet with manacles, buffeted your cheeks, spat upon your face, blinded thine eyes, so that all your senses, when they should have been refreshed, were afflicted. Oh how far did these matins differ from those, which, at the same time, the blessed angels did sing in heaven? They cried holy, holy, and the Jews cried, he is guilty of death, crucify, crucify him. O angelic spirits which understand both cries, what could you imagine or think when you saw the inhuman cruelty wherewith he was handled on earth, whom in heaven you adored with such great submission and reverence? Did you not wonder to see him suffer all these extreme torments, to expiate the sins of those who inflicted them upon him? Who has ever heard of such immense charity, that for this reason one should suffer death, to heal the grief and cure the wounds of his murderers?

The fall of St. Peter, that great pillar, did not a little increase the anxiety of this tedious night; that he, whom he [Christ] entirely loved amongst the rest, whom he chose to present at his glorious transfiguration, to whom he committed the primacy of his holy Church, whom he ordained to be head and prince of the Apostles, that he, I say, should before his face and in his presence, deny him, not once but thrice, adding blasphemies and oaths, that he knew not the man. Tell me, Peter, did this man seem to you so ungodly and wicked that in future times you did fear it would be a disgrace unto you to confess him now? Did you not consider that you did first pronounce the sentence of condemnation against him before he was adjudged by the high priests when you did not esteem him so much as worthy of your acknowledgment? Could you do a greater injury to Jesus Christ?

But Christ, sorrowful for this great fault of St. Peter, turned himself and cast his eyes upon him, that with his gracious countenance he might reduce this wandering sheep into the sheepfold of his mercies. O admirable aspect, secret indeed, but full of signification, which St. Peter knew right well and well understood of what force and efficacy it was. The crowing of the cock had little availed to his compunction and conversion, had not the countenance of Christ our Savior been adjoined; whose eyes did speak and work that stupendous change, the certainty of which not only the flowing tears of St. Peter, but of our Blessed Savior himself did sufficiently testify. After all these injuries, consider what Christ suffered when he was bound to be scourged at the pillar for the judge, when he saw that he could not pacify the fury of those infernal monsters, thought good to advise them to beat him with rods and whips, whereby his whole body might be torn, hoping that way to mollify their obstinate and obdurate hearts; that when they saw him so torn and mangled, they would cease further to desire his cruel death.

Enter now, my soul, in spirit, into the house of Pilate, and have tears in readiness, for you will have need of them if you will diligently consider what was done there.

Behold, how inhumanly these abject and infamous rogues despoiled our Blessed Savior of his garments. Mark the humility of Christ, how he suffered himself to be stripped, not so much as opening his mouth, nor uttering any word against their injurious behaviour. See his sacred body bound to the pillar with many ropes in such a fashion that on every side they might have room to torture him. Consider how the Lord of angels stood alone in the midst of his cruel enemies, without any advocates, or procurators that would defend his cause, yea, altogether without any one man, who, at leastwise, afar off, would so much as compassionate the bitterness of his torments. Do you not hear the noise of rods and whips, wherewith they loaded, tore, and rent the delicate flesh of Jesus, adding stroke upon stroke and wound to wound? Do you not see his whole body in one short moment of time with the vehemency and often reiterated blows, to be covered, as it were, with one ulcer, his skin to be drawn from the flesh and blood from his whole body, from the crown of his head to the soles of his feet, to flow down upon the earth? Especially, is it not dreadful for you to behold the place between the shoulders, whereupon almost the whole force of the blows did light? Consider how Christ, the Savior of the world, after that extreme cruelty of his tormentors, went up and down the palace all torn and cut, seeking and gathering up his garments, not finding one amongst those inhuman rascals that would show unto him the least act of humanity, in washing or refreshing his wounds, or lend their hand to help him to put on his clothes. All these things are worthy of our diligent consideration, that thereby we might stir up our souls to due compassion of his miseries.

A Meditation for Thursday—On the Crowning with Thorns, the Ecce Homo, and the Carrying of the Cross

This day you will meditate how Christ was crowned with thorns; his presentation before all the people; his condemnation; his bringing out to the place of execution; and, last of all, his carrying of his Cross. The spouse in the Canticles invited us to the consideration of these torments, when she said, "Go forth, ye daughters of Sion, and see king Solomon in the diadem, wherewith his mother crowned him in the day of his espousals, and in the day of the joy of his heart" (Song 3:11).

What do you do? What do you think, my soul? My tongue, why are you silent? O sweet Savior, when I open my eyes and behold this sorrowful spectacle, my heart is rent with grief. What, Lord, were not your former torments, imminent death, and abundance of your blood already shed sufficient for the redemption of mankind? But you must yet be crowned with sharp thorns? My soul, that you may the better understand this sad spectacle set before thine eyes, our Blessed Savior in his former beauty, before he suffered these torments, then behold him, on the contrary, in this miserable state. If in the first you do rightly view him, you will see him more beautiful than the sun: in his eyes a comely gravity; in his speech a gracious facility; in his actions singular modesty; in the gesture of his whole body profound humility joined with reverend majesty.

Then, after you have satiated your soul with pleasure, in beholding this rare piece of admirable perfection, then turn thine eyes again and look upon him as he is, in this present miserable state. Ridiculously clothed in purple, bearing in his hand a reed for a kingly sceptre and upon his head a crown of sharp thorns instead of a regal diadem. His eyes were dimmed, his face pale and wan, fouled and covered with the filthy spittle of his own people; behold him within and without! His heart consumed with grief, his body torn with wounds and blows, forsaken of his disciples, hastened to undergo death from his enemies, mocked of the soldiers, despised of the high priests, rejected as a wicked king arrogantly assuming this title, unjustly accused and destitute of all human aid. Do not consider these things as done and past many years since, but imagine with yourself, that at this present time they are acting before your face, not as another man's sorrows, but as thine own afflictions. Set yourself in his place, and conjecture what torments you should suffer if your head were bored to the skull and your brain pierced with sharp thorns? But what do I say, thorns? When you can scarce endure the prick of a small needle? How great, then, was the pain his tender head suffered, with this new and unheard-of torment?

The coronation of our Blessed Savior, with many mocks and scorns concluded, the judge produced him before the people, saying: "Behold the man." If you thirst after the death of the man, behold him scarce a hair's breadth distant from it; yes, he is brought to that pass, that he deserves rather commiseration than your envy. If you fear that he will make himself king, behold, he is so deformed that he scarcely retains the shape of a man: do you fear any violence from these hands that are so straightly manacled? Do you dread any harm from a man that is cast into such a miserable and dejected state, whose body is so mangled and weakened? Consider, O my soul, in what state your Savior was when the very judge himself did think that this aspect would move his bloody enemies to compassion; from which we may gather what a miserable thing it is to see a Christian of such an obdurate heart, which cannot or will not condole with the sufferings of our Savior, when they were such that the very judge did think them sufficient to mollify the malice of his enemies. But Pilate, seeing with these exceeding torments he could no way temper or assuage their fury, went into his palace and sat in the judgment seat to pronounce the definitive sentence against Christ. Now the Cross was prepared at the door and the fatal standard which threatened ruin to our Blessed Savior was now in readiness.

The sentence being pronounced, with the addition of more torments, they loaded his wearied shoulders with a heavy cross to carry to the place of his execution. But our meek Lord not only not rejected it, but out of that immense charity towards us, wherewith he suffered for our sins, obediently and willingly embraced it. Now the innocent Isaac, with his weak shoulders, supported the intolerable burden of the Cross to the place of sacrifice. The simple people and devout women followed him weeping. For who was able to contain tears, to see the Lord and King of angels going thus on foot, with the extremity of torments? His knees quivering, his body stooping, his eyes blinded, his face besmeared with blood, his head crowned with thorns, and his ears deafened with the noise of drums and trumpets. Leave awhile, O my soul, this horrid spectacle, and with watering eyes, with sobs and sighs, go to the Blessed Virgin and say to her: Lady of Angels, Queen of Heaven, Gate of Paradise, Advocate of the World, Sanctuary of Sinners, Health of the Just, Joy of the Saints, Mistress of Virtue, Mirror of Purity, Symbol of Chastity, Pattern of Patience, and Rule of all Perfection. O me, miserable and unfortunate, what have I seen with the eyes of faith? How could I live to behold such inhuman usage? Interrupting sighs will not permit me scarce to speak how I left your only begotten Son, loaded with a mighty cross, to which he was presently to be nailed and carrying it to the place of execution.

What heart, what mind, what soul is able to comprehend the profound grief the Blessed Virgin Mary then did suffer? Her heart fainted and a dead sweat with extreme anguish possessed her whole body, and presently she had given up the ghost, had not the divine dispensation reserved her till better times, for her greater merit and more abundant reward. The Blessed Virgin with speed followed the steps of her Beloved Son; that ardent desire wherewith she was inflamed to see him added vigor to her, of which sorrow had bereft her. She heard afar off the noise of arms, the concourse of people, and the sound of trumpets on every side, publishing the Passion of Christ. After that, she saw the glittering of lances and halberds; in the way she found his footsteps sprinkled with drops of blood, by which, without any guide or leader, she might easily find the way. Approaching to her Son, she lifted up her eyes swelled with tears, to behold him whom she esteemed dearer than her own soul.

Oh what strife was there in the soul of this Blessed Virgin between fear and love? She did vehemently desire to see her Son, but, on the other side, she dared not cast her eyes upon him in this lamentable and afflicted state. At length, when she drew nearer, these two celestial lights beheld each other, their eyes pierced each other's souls, but grief enforced their tongues to silence; notwithstanding, their hearts did mutually discourse and the Son unto the mother said: Sweet mother, why comest thou hither, my love, O my dove? Your sorrow renews my miseries and my torments crucify your soul! Return, return again into your house; this defiled company of thieves and murderers sees not your virginal purity. These and like words they inwardly uttered all the way until they came to the place of execution.

A Meditation for Friday—On the Crucifixion and the Seven Last Words on the Cross

This day you will meditate upon the mystery of the Cross and the seven words which Christ spoke upon it. Rouse up, my soul, and duly ponder this great mystery of the Cross which brought forth the fruit of satisfaction, to expiate that great loss which all mankind suffered by a tree. Consider how, before our Blessed Savior came to the Mount of Calvary, (to make his death more ignominious) his cruel tormentors stripped him of all his clothes except his coat which was without seam. Behold how patiently this meek lamb suffers his garments to be taken from him, not so much as opening his mouth or speaking one word against their barbarous dealing. He permitted these things willingly, but with a great strain to modesty. He was stripped naked that we might receive a better garment to cover the nakedness of our sins than that which Adam, the first parent of all mankind, made of the leaves of fig trees to cover the nakedness of his body. Some doctors think that the crown of thorns was taken off, to pull with more facility his unseamed garment over his ears, and after to be fastened on again, which could not be without a vehement pain; the sharp thorns did afresh wound his sacred head with unspeakable torment. And surely this is not unlikely, seeing in the whole time of his Passion they spared him in nothing; but the bitterest torments they could devise, they heaped upon him, especially when the Evangelist saith, they did to him whatsoever they would. This coat did so cleave to the wounds of his sacred body, by reason of the congealed blood, that when the barbarous hangmen ripped It off with exceeding violence, they reopened again the wounds of Jesus; they pulled off with it many particles of flesh, so that the whole body of Christ, in every part flayed and bloody from the head to the foot, seemed to be but one entire and continuous wound.

Weigh well with yourself, my soul, the immense goodness and mercy of God manifested in these torments; behold, him that spreads the heavens with clouds, clothes the green and pleasant fields with flowers, and he, that liberally bestows clothing upon every creature, behold him, I say, stark naked! Consider what cold this precious body, being wounded, suffered; when they had not only despoiled him of his garments, but his very skin was not entire, neither were his wounds bound up, but exposed to the injury of the air. If St. Peter, being well clothed, could not overcome the cold of the forepassed night, what cold do you think this delicate body suffered, being in every place wounded and all naked? Then, consider how Christ was fastened to the Cross, and what torment he suffered when the sharp nails pierced the most sensible parts of his tender body. Weigh, with yourself that the Blessed Virgin, who beheld these things with her eyes, and hearing the frequent blows of the mallet in driving the nails into the hands and feet of her Son, was not insensible, but that the heart of the Mother was pierced with the hands and feet of the Son. When Christ was made fast upon the Cross, presently they lifted it up and put it into a hole, there before prepared; behold how these wicked torturers of the innocent Jesus, pricked forward with their own malice, let the heavy Cross fall into the hole with such violence, that it so much strained his body, hanging only by the nails, and rent wider the wounds of his hands and feet.

Sweet Savior, can there be found a heart so hard and steely, which is not filled with empathy at such a spectacle, when the very stones did cleave asunder, as sensible of your cruel torments? O Lord, the pains of death compassed you round about; the storms and waves of the raging sea surrounded you on every side; the waters entered into your soul; you didst descend to the deep abyss where you could find no footing. When your heavenly Father did forsake you Lord, what could you expect your enemies would do? They cried out against you, and your friends did wound your heart; your soul was sad and heavy, neither was there any that would comfort you. Lord, from these unheard-of torments and abundant satisfaction which you madest for my sins, I cannot but acknowledge, with all humility, the grievousness of my heinous transgressions, which were the occasions of all your miseries. I see you, my King and God, fastened upon a wooden cross with two iron nails; your precious and tender flesh to be stretched without any manner of respite. If you would a little ease yourself upon your heel, the weight of your whole body enlarges their wounds. If you would leave the burthen to your hands, the weight of it does likewise rend their wounds. Your sacred head could find no rest, because you had no other pillow than the sharp crown of thorns.

O Virgin Mother, how willingly would you have embraced him in your arms, thereon to ease and rest himself a little, but the arms of the Cross would not permit you, upon which, if he would repose, the sharp thorns struck deeper into his head. The troubles of the Son were much augmented by the presence of the Mother, which no less crucified his soul than the Jews his body to the Cross. O sweet Jesus, in one day you did carry a double cross, the one upon your body, the other in your soul; the one of passion, the other of compassion; the one pierced your body with nails of iron, the other your soul with nails of sorrow. What tongue is able to express what you did suffer to see the anguish of your dear Mother, whose soul you did certainly know to be crucified together with you, when you beheld her heavy heart, pierced with the sword of sorrow? When with bloody eyes you looked upon her beautiful face, pale and wan, and didst hear the sighs of her dying soul, lamenting that she could not die? What did you suffer to see pure fountains of tears gushing from her eyes and to hear her pitiful complaints she made in sorrowing for your sufferings?

Then, consider, the seven words which Christ spoke upon the Cross to his heavenly Father, saying, "Father forgive them, for they know not what they do." To the thief: "This day thou shalt be with me in paradise." To his Mother: "Woman behold thy Son." To the people he said: "I thirst." And to God again: "My God, my God, why hast thou forsaken me?" "It is consummated." "Into thy hands I commend my spirit." Ruminate, my soul, with what exceeding charity he made intercession to his heavenly Father for his enemies and persecutors; with what piety and mercy he received the penitent thief into his favor; with what affection he committed his mother to the protection of his beloved disciple; with what ardor he testified himself vehemently to thirst after the salvation of mankind; with what clamor he thundered out his prayer, expressing to the divine Majesty the grievousness of his tribulations; how perfectly he fulfilled the obedience enjoined to him by his heavenly Father; and lastly, how he yielded his soul into his blessed hands.

Every one of which words do afford us a great deal of matter for our instruction; in the first, we are taught to love our enemies; in the second, mercy towards sinners; in the third, piety towards our parents; in the fourth, to thirst after our neighbour's salvation; in the fifth, when we are oppressed with tribulations, and seeming, as it were, to be left of God, to fly to prayer; in the sixth, the virtue of obedience and perseverance; in the seventh, perfect resignation into the hands of God, which is the sum of all perfection.

A Meditation for Saturday—On the Piercing with the Lance, the Taking Down from the Cross, the Sorrows of Mary, and the Burial

This day you will meditate upon the piercing of our Blessed Savior's side with a spear; the taking down of Christ from the Cross; the lamentations of the women; and other things which did occur about his burial. First, take notice, how that Christ, after he gave up his spirit upon the Cross, his enemies much rejoiced at his death. But yet, there was not an end of their insatiate cruelty, but still their increasing malice raged against him, being dead. They divided and cast lots for his garments, and with a spear pierced his precious side. O barbarous infidels! O stone hearts! Did you think those torments he suffered before his death were not sufficient that you would not vouchsafe to spare him, being dead? What madness did possess your souls? Lift up your eyes and behold his dead face, his eyes sunk, his hanging head, and his whole body being wan and pale. Although your hearts be harder than adamant, yet let this pitiful aspect mollify them.

Behold the centurion struck a lance into his sacred side with such violence that the very Cross did tremble, out of whose side did gush abundance of blood and water, for the redemption of all mankind. O river of paradise, running forth to water the whole earth! O precious wound which rather the love you did bear for us sinful men than the enemies' weapon did inflict! O gate of heaven, window of paradise, place of rest, tower of fortitude, sanctuary of the just, nest of doves, tomb of pilgrims, flourishing bed of the spouse! Hail, sacred wound, which pierces devout hearts; hail, rose of incredible beauty; hail, precious stone of inestimable valor; hail, door, through which lies open a free passage to the heart of Christ, an argument of his love, and pledge of eternal felicity! Consider, that in the evening, Joseph and Nicodemus came with ladders to loose and take down the body of our Savior; but the Blessed Virgin, after all these torments, perceiving her Son to be taken from the cross and disposed for the grave, she took him, when he was let down, in her arms, humbly beseeching that holy company that they would suffer her to come near his body and to bestow her last kiss and embracings upon him, which upon the Cross she could not do, which they would not, nor could deny; for if her friends had deprived her of him dead, which her enemies did her of him living, they had redoubled the anguish of her soul.

When she saw her Son in this case, what grief, what tortures can we imagine she then did suffer? Angels of peace, come and lament with this blessed Virgin; lament heaven, lament stars, lament all creatures of the world. She embraced the mangled body of her Beloved Son; she hugged him in her arms, (for love administered this strength); she thrust her face amongst the thorns to come to kiss his mouth, whereby she wounded her face with the sharp pricks which she washed with flowing tears. O sweet Mother, is this your Beloved Son? Is this he whom you conceived with great glory and brought forth with great joy? Is this that bright mirror in which you were wont to see yourself? All that were present did likewise mourn, the other Marys which were there mourned, the noblemen lamented, heaven and earth with all creatures mourned with the Blessed Virgin.

That holy Evangelist lamented, who often embracing the body of his dear Master, saying, O my good Lord and Master, who shall hereafter teach and instruct me? With whom now shall I consult on doubtful occasions? Upon whose lap shall I now rest myself? Who shall now reveal unto me celestial secrets? What sudden change is this? Yesterday I rested upon your sacred breast, where you didst communicate to me the joys and glory of everlasting life, and now in recompense of that benefit I embrace you dead in my arms? Is this that countenance which I beheld glorious and transfigured upon the mount of Thabor? Is this that face which I saw brighter and more glittering than the sun? And that Blessed sinner, St. Mary Magdalene lamented, who often kissing the feet of her Savior, saying, O the true light of mine eyes, the only remedy and solace of my soul. If I sin again, who shall hereafter receive me into favor? Who shall defend me from the calumnies of the Pharisees? O how altered are these feet from those washed with my tears! O beloved of my heart, why do I not die with you? O life of my soul, how can I say I love you, when I, living, see you dead before me? Thus, this blessed company did mourn and lament, watering with abundant tears the body of Jesus. The sepulchre being ready, they spiced his holy body with sweet spices, they wrapped it up in a fine linen cloth, bound his head with a handkerchief, laid it upon a bier, carried it to the place of burial and put it into a new monument. The monument was covered with a stone and the face of Mary obscured with a cloud of sorrow. When there again she bade her Son adieu, she then began to be more and more sensible of her solitude; for, then, she saw herself to be deprived of the greatest good. But her heart remained buried with her treasure in the grave.

A Meditation for Sunday—On the Decent into Hell, the Appearances of Our Lord, and His Ascension

This day you will consider and meditate of the descent of Christ to hell; his Resurrection; divers apparitions to the Blessed Virgin Mary; St. Mary Magdalen, and his other disciples; and last of all, his glorious Ascension into heaven. Take notice, therefore, of the incredible joy the Fathers, which were detained in hell, felt at the coming of the Redeemer, who came to free them from the dark prison, wherein they were shut for many thousand years. What prayers, what giving of thanks, did they render to him who had brought them to the long desired haven of their salvation? They who return from the East Indies are wont to say that they think all their forepassed labors well bestowed only for that joy they find the first day of their arrival into their country. If the banishment of a year or two and the tediousness of a little troublesome journey can breed such joy in men, what will the absence of three or four thousand years do from that pleasant and celestial country! What joy, therefore, do we think those holy Fathers had, when they took possession of it?

Then, consider the excessive joy of the Blessed Virgin, when she saw her Son risen from death, when it is most certain and undoubted that she felt the greatest sorrow and affliction that could be at the ignominious death and Passion, her joy must needs excel the rest, in his triumphant Resurrection. How great do you think was her content and pleasure to see her Son, whom she grievously lamented before his death, living glorious and attended with a joyful troop of holy patriarchs, whom he brought along with him? What did she say? What did she do? With what kisses did she salute him? With what affection did she embrace him? What pleasant rivers of tears distilled from her eyes? How earnestly did she desire to follow her Son, had it been permitted to her? Moreover, take notice, of the joy of the holy Marys, particularly of her who stood weeping at the sepulchre of Christ, when, without doubt, she saw him whom her soul loved, she cast herself at his feet when she beheld him living, whom she sought amongst the dead. After his Mother, he therefore appeared to her, who loved him most ardently, and, above others, sought him most diligently and perseveringly, to instruct us that when we look for God, we must seek him with tears and diligence.

Consider that after this, he appeared to his disciples going to Emmaus in the habit of a pilgrim; behold how courteously he joined himself a companion to them; how familiarly he conversed with them; how handsomely he dissembled his person; and after, with what affection he manifested himself unto them; and last of all, how he left their tongues, and lips, filled with the delightful discourse of his Majesty. Let your discourse and talk be like these disciples, as they travelled in the way, of the love and Passion of our Blessed Savior; and, I dare be bold to say that he will not deny unto you his sacred presence.

In the mystery of our Blessed Savior's Ascension, first, consider that he deferred it for forty days, that in the meantime, often appearing to his disciples, he might instruct them, and with them discourse of the kingdom of heaven; for he would not forsake them by ascending into heaven before he had disposed their minds to ascend with him spiritually. Hence we may note, those that are often deprived of the corporal presence of Christ, and of sensible devotion, who, with the wings of contemplation, fly up to heaven and fear no danger. Wherein the divine providence, wherewith it curbs and governs the elect, does wonderfully manifest itself, how it strengthens the weak, exercises the strong, gives milk to little ones, prepares stronger meat for great ones, comforts some, afflicts others, and to conclude, accommodates himself to all according to their several degrees in their spiritual profit.

Wherefore, he that is strengthened by divine comfort, ought, therefore, not to presume of himself, seeing this sensible consolation is but the nourishment for infirm ones and a great sign of weakness; nor he that is exercised by affliction, ought, therefore, to be dejected, seeing temptation is for the most part a testimony of a valiant mind. Christ ascended up to heaven in the presence of his disciples, that they might be witnesses of this mystery of which they were beholders; no one can give better testimony to Almighty God's deeds, than he who has learned them by experience; wherefore, he that would certainly know how good, how sweet and merciful he is towards his, and what is the force and efficacy of his divine grace, love, providence, and spiritual consolations, let him ask those who indeed have had experience of them, for they, and only they, will give him the best instructions and satisfaction.

Moreover, Christ would ascend, his disciples looking upon him, that they might pursue him with their eyes and spirit, that they might have a cordial feeling of his departure, that in his absence they might fear to remain alone, and that they might the better dispose themselves to receive his holy grace. The prophet Eliseus, when Elias was to be taken and separated from him, desired that he would give his spirit. Elias made answer: "Thou hast asked a hard thing; nevertheless, if thou see me when I am taken from thee, thou shalt have what thou hast asked; but if thou see me not, thou shalt not have it" (2 Kings 2:10).

In like manner, they shall be heirs of the spirit of Christ, whom love does cause to mourn for his departure; to whom his absence seems grievous, who earnestly, while they live in this banishment, desire his holy presence. Such a saint was he that said, you are gone, my comforter, without any care of me, at your departure you did bless your own and I saw it not; the angels promised that you should return again and I heard them not. Who is able to express or understand the solitude, trouble, cries, and tears of the Blessed Virgin, of his beloved disciple, St. Mary Magdalene, and the other Apostles, when they saw Christ to be taken from them, who, together with him, carried up their affectionate hearts? And yet, notwithstanding, it is said of them that they returned with great joy into Jerusalem; the same love and affection which made them bewail the visible loss of their beloved Lord and Master, did likewise cause that they congratulated each other, much rejoicing at his glory, for it is the nature of true love not so much to seek the commodity of itself as the honor and commodity of the person that is beloved. Last of all, to close up this meditation, it is left to us to consider with what glory, with what joy, this noble conqueror was brought into that heavenly city; what solemnities were then instituted in the glorious paradise; how magnificently was he entertained by those celestial citizens? What a delightful spectacle was it to see men accompanied with angels, to go in procession, and to sit upon those seats which for many thousand years were vacant. But a most ravishing joy it was, to behold the sacred humanity of Jesus Christ, transcending all others, to sit at the right hand of his eternal Father. All these things are worthy of your attentive consideration, that you may learn, that the labors you do undergo for the love of God are not spent in vain, therefore, he that humbled himself under all creatures, it was requisite that he should be exalted above all, that the lovers of true glory may trace this path; they must expect if they desire to be above all, that first they be subject to all, even their inferiors.

APPENDIX

QUOTES OF ST. PETER OF ALCANTARA

"Let him who desires to advance on the road to virtue not start without the spur of devotion; for otherwise he will altogether fail to make his stumbling, ill-conditioned beast hold up."

"It is as necessary to regulate the heart before prayer and meditation as to tune the guitar before playing it."

"In prayer the soul renews its youth and regains its freshness."

"Beware of spending so much time in devotional reading as thereby to hinder devout meditation, this last being a more fruitful exercise, inasmuch as those things on which we attentively reflect sink deeper and produce greater results."

"In meditation let the person rouse himself from things temporal, and let him collect himself within himself, that is to say, within the very centre of his soul, where lies impressed the image of God. Here let him hearken to the voice of God as though speaking to him from on high, yet present in his soul, and as though there were no other in the world save God and himself."

"In meditation we must act like a wise gardener who, when he waters a plot of ground, waits a while after the first sprinkling of water until it be soaked in, and then sprinkles again, so that the earth may be thoroughly wet and thus become more fruitful."

"We must use special caution in speaking to others of those hidden consolations with which Almighty God has been pleased to refresh our souls. Even as that mellifluous doctor—St. Bernard—was wont to advise everyone to have these words in large letters written in his room, 'My secret TO MYSELF.'"

BRIEF RELATION OF THE LIFE AND DEATH OF THE BLESSED FATHER, FR. PETER DE ALCANTARA, FRANCISCAN FRIAR, WRITTEN BY GILES WILLOUGHBY, OF THE SAME ORDER AND OBSERVANCE

"The mercies of the Lord I will sing for ever" (Ps 88:1) saith that kingly Prophet David. And not without cause; for, so great and unspeakable are the mercy-works of the Almighty, which out of the bowels of his infinite goodness he hath shewed to mankind, from the first instant of his creation, that the tongues of men and angels are never able to express them. How wonderful was this benefit, that creating man after his own image and likeness (Gen 1:26)[1] he would have made him partaker of eternal felicity, and vested with his original justice without death,[2] or any passage by misery, would have associated him with the company of angels, if he had not, by his own default, violated the laws of his creator. Notwithstanding this act of malice, the divine clemency would not suffer the work of his powerful hands so to perish, but he, according to the diversity of times,[3] always ordained opportune remedies, to reduce wandering man to the right way of his own salvation. Now manifesting his divine pleasure, by the means of angels; now sending the patriarchs replenished with his heavenly grace, who by their good example, might stir them up to piety; then sending the prophets illuminated with his Holy Spirit, not only to preach the present benefits exhibited to mankind, but also to foretell the future incarnation of the Son of God, with the mystery of his death and Passion, by means of which, man should be loosed from the power of Satan and eased of the heavy load of his transgressions.

---

1. The Teacher [Peter Lombard], *Sentences*, Bk. 3, Distinction 20.
2. Gabriel, Bk. 2, Distinction 19, single question, Article 2.
3. John Duns Scotus, Bk. 4, Distinction 1, Question 7, Number 2.

Thus far hath that impenetrable abyss of the divine clemency sweetly disposed all things, requisite for the saving of the soul of man. But if we will extend our thoughts a little further, and call to mind the great benefits still heaped upon man after the Ascension of our Blessed Savior, we shall find them innumerable. Who is not astonished at the vocation of mankind, that the apostolical trumpet of a few men, sounding to human ears the evangelical truth, through the whole world, shall rouse up[4] souls, making them[5] happy, and thrice happy, to forsake all worldly vanities? To betake themselves to a state of perfection; to sell all they have and give to the poor; to live in perpetual chastity, and simple obedience; to spend their days in rigorous penance, watching, fasting, and prayer; and finally to renounce all the seeming pleasures, for true there are none[6] which the flattering world could afford unto them.

These things are daily put in practice by many who profess the gospel of Christ. For, where Catholic religion flourisheth, we see divers monasteries of men and women filled with religious souls, who consecrate themselves a perpetual sacrifice to the Almighty. How many religious do we see honored with priestly function, an office requiring more than human purity[7], and a burthen scarcely to be supported by angel's

---

4. (Religious) [are] the more elite and wiser part of the Church. Indeed these must be considered wiser than the rest of the crowd of mortals since they have separated themselves from the society of the world so that they might consecrate their life to God. Gregory Nazienzien, *Oration in Praise of St. Basil.*

5. Indeed those are blessed, and thrice blessed, as ones who have burned with the love of God, and on account of his love might have considered all things as nothing. Indeed, they have poured forth tears, and day and night they have spent in lamentation, so that they might obtain eternal consolation. They have tamed their flesh with hunger and thirst and vigils, so that in that place the delights and joys of paradise might receive them. Damascene, in the *Story of Saint Josaphat.*

6. The consolation of the world is cheap, and useful for nothing, and what is more to be feared it is an impediment to true and healthy consolation. St. Bernard in "Sermon 4 on the vigil of the Birth of the Lord." All things under the sun are in this state that nothing in them is truly pleasurable. Indeed the solution to every problem is the beginning of another problem. Similarly in the "Sermon on the Beginning, Middle, and Last Things." See more in Jerome Platus *On the Good of the Religious State*, Bk. 1, sec. 3, ch. 1.

7. How can one enjoying the benefits of such a sacrifice not be purer? How can the hand which breaks this flesh not be more splendid than the rays of the sun, or the mouth which is filled with the fire of the spirit, or the tongue which is reddened with the awe-inspiring blood? St. John Chrysostom, *Homily 83 on Matthew.* And Pope Gelasius, writing to Bishop Alpidius, doth excellently set down the great purity required to priestly function saying, "The holy service of God which includes the practice of the Catholic faith demands for itself so much reverance for itself that no one should dare to approach it unless with a pure conscience. For how should the heavenly spirit descend, having been invoked for the consecration of the divine mystery, if even the priest who prays for it to be present be condemned, full of shameful deeds." Bk. 1, question 1, ch. on the Sacred. Although a wicked priest doth consecrate and administer the sacraments truly, yet he sinneth grievously in consecrating and administering unworthily: "The sacrifices of the unjust will be an obstacle to the very ones who shamelessly offer them." Bk. 1, question 1, ch. on Isaiah. It

Appendix

shoulders, executing their charge with great integrity of mind, careful of their own, and zealous of the saving of their neighbours' souls; who, by their holy doctrine and exemplary lives, preach to the Christian world a reformation; who spare no pains or tedious travels to propagate the faith of Jesus Christ to heathens and infidels; who courageously labor in Almighty God's vineyard, exposing their lives for the name of Jesus.

The Indies, both East and West, are witnesses of their zealous and heroic spirits, there they sealed the truth of the gospel with the effusion of their sacred blood; yea, what acts memorable in the Church of God are there, wherein[8] these men have not had a very great stroke? And, finally, they so well employ and multiply those talents which the great Commander of heaven and earth hath bestowed upon them here, that assuredly they may expect an eternal reward in the kingdom of heaven hereafter. But that which is more admirable to see, a multitude of the weaker sex abandon all worldly pleasures; they who in the world might have swum in bravery, and have had all things at their own command, to enclose themselves in a retired cloister, there to spend their days in penance, and to consecrate the very flower of their springing youth a sweet-smelling sacrifice to their celestial spouse, Jesus Christ. These, truly, are those that[9] fill and beautify the garden of paradise with lilies of purity; these are the flowers[10] of our holy mother, the Catholic Church, which make her glorious and fruitful. These are they that make that happy change, a moment's fading pleasure for an immortal crown of glory.

Thus we see perpetual rivers streaming from the fountain of Almighty God's mercy. But let us descend a little further into his abun-

---

is necessary that the hand which seeks to wash off dirt, make an effort to be itself clean; lest if it itself is filthy covered with the mud of manure it further sully all it touches. St. Gregory in Bk. 1, part 1, letter 24; also cited in Bk. 1, question 1, ch. "It is Necessary."

8. Fr. Jerome Platus, S.J., *On the Happiness of the Religious State*, vol. 1, part 2, ch. 30.

9. Marriages fill the earth; virginity fills paradise. St Jerome.

10. That is the flower of the ecclesiastical seed, the glory and ornament of spiritual grace, a joyful disposition, a complete and incorrupt work of praise and honor, an image of God corresponding to the holiness of the Lord, the more illustrious portion of the flock of Christ. The glorious fruitfulness of Holy Mother Church rejoices because of these, and in these the she flourishes more widely. The more glorious Virginity adds to her number, the more the joy of the mother increases. Cyprian, *On the Dress of Virgins*, Bk. 1, part 4, ch. 24.

117

dant charity, and take notice of his Fatherly providence, that in process of declining times, when the blood of our Redeemer hath often begun to wax cold in the hearts of men, he would not suffer it altogether to be extinguished, but according to variety of times, never ceased to repair his Church by the ministry of some elected servants whom he sent into this world as second Apostles, who by their example and doctrine might draw men out of the mire of their sins, renew the fervour of our Blessed Savior's Passion, and reduce collapsed discipline to her former rigor. Many hath he sent for this end, and amongst many this blessed Saint, St. Peter de Alcantara, a man, from his very cradle, consecrated to evangelical perfection; he was a faithful laborer in our Lord's vineyard, with great fidelity performing his commanded task, as it will plainly appear by that which followeth in his life.

Of the Birth and Education of Blessed Alcantara and of His Entering into Religion

This blessed Saint was born at Norba Cæsarea,[11] vulgarly called Alcantara, in the year of our Lord 1449, in the reign of Pope Alexander VI, and Ferdinando, Catholic King of Spain. His father was called Bachilier Garavito, and his mother Maria Villela de Senabria, both of good quality, but especially honored for their virtues. They brought up their young son in the fear of God and sowed in him the seeds of virtue; they put him to school where, as he profited in learning, so his obedience towards his parents did likewise increase. Although he was a child, yet he withdrew himself from the common sports of children and sorted himself amongst men, whom he saw inclined to devotion. In these his tender years, he addicted himself to the works of mercy. He applied himself seriously to learn the Christian doctrine. He often visited churches and holy places. He frequented the sacraments and continually employed

---

11. A famous military state of Spain of the Alcantarene order. This order insofar as it consists of a privilege was granted to it in the year of Our Lord 1174, and was established by Lord Gomesius Hernandes in the time of King Ferdinand II and was approved by Alexander III, Lucius III,, and Innocent IV. Rod Questions Reg. Vol. 1, Question 4, Article 4 [Emmanuel Rodriguez, Regular Questions Explained (Regulares Quaestiones Enucleatae)].

himself in good works, all which did abundantly presage his future sanctity; but more confirmed it, by that which followed immediately, for he was scarce sixteen years of age, when, before he knew, he began to loath the world, and when the young sparks of his virtues began to break into a flame of devotion. He opened the doors of his soul to the inspirations of the Holy Ghost, and as he excelled his fellow students in science, so he knew that all science was ignorance without the right knowledge of God.[12] Therefore, from that time forward he applied his mind to heavenly wisdom and busied himself chiefly to know what should be most acceptable to his Sacred Majesty.

About that time, there was a famous and reformed monastery of Franciscans in the province of St. Gabriel, three miles from Valentia, whither he addressed himself, there to bring his good desires to a joyful period. But as he went along towards this place, he came to a great river, called Tiartar, which, without boat, was impossible to be passed over. He seeing this unexpected bar to stop his happy journey, looked about, hoping to espy some waterman who might carry him over, but when he could see none to give him any assistance, he cast his eyes to heaven and with great anxiety lamented this unhappy hindrance. Behold! upon the sudden (as he himself related,)[13] he was miraculously transported on the other side of the river, without any notable motion that he could perceive. This miracle was not unlike to that when the river Jordan stood still for the children of Israel to pass; or when St. Peter walked upon the waves of the sea; and, indeed, it was no small beginning of Almighty God's many favors exhibited to this blessed Saint. This obstacle being removed, he passed the other part of his way (the Holy Ghost being his guide) without any difficulty, and at length arrived to his desired harbor, this solitary monastery, situated amongst great rocks, which they commonly call Los Manxeredes, where he came to the fathers and asked the habit of St. Francis of them, who did grant it to him with as much

---

12. What would it profit him to know those things which ought to be done who does not continue to the work? From Chrysostom, *Homily 13 on Romans.*

13. Marianus, *Life of St. Peter of Alcantara,* ch. 1.

charity as he begged it with humility. But, when this blessed Saint considered his poor habitation, sequestered from the company of men, and abstracted from all worldly tumults, and when he saw himself vested in his penitential weed, we may well imagine with what meditations he spurred himself forward in Almighty God's service.

He spake to his own soul these or the like words: behold, thou hast now accomplished thy desire, thou art now arrived to the land of promise and climbed up to the highest mountain[14] of Almighty God's favor to mortal man in this vale of misery, (that is), the sacred state of a religious life, where, by how much more thou art sequestered from the pleasures of the flattering world, the more thou enjoyest the freedom of thy spirit. Thou art now come to the house of God, in which it is better for thee to be an abject than to dwell in the courts of princes. All occasions of offending thy Creator are now taken away; thy soul is now sure not to be defiled with the pitch of evil conversation. Thy company now are[15] terrestrial angels, who, though they live on earth, yet they have their conversation in heaven, all whose actions incite thee to nothing else but to aspire unto perfection. Thou findest here no snares to entangle thee into worldly vanities, no flatterers to applaud thee when thou dost offend, or anything else to withdraw thy affection from the Cross of Christ.

Thy beloved spouse hath brought thee now into this holy desert, to recreate thy soul with his heavenly consolations[16] here abstracted from all worldly tumults; it may attend only to divine wisdom; and the noise of all temporal cares being hushed and silent, it may be wholly employed in sacred contemplation and ravished with eternal pleasures. Almighty God hath now wafted thee over this troublesome sea and placed thee here, in the quiet harbor of thy salvation, in which state, in respect of

---

14. As much as this mountainous land, placed on high, is free from the delights of the world, so much does it have the greater delights of the spirit. St Jerome, Bk. 1, ch. 2 of the Epistles, Letter 8 to Eustochium.

15. I do not know by what name I should call them, whether heavenly men or earthly angels, passing their time on the earth but having their abode in the heavens. St. Bernard, *Sermon to the Brothers of Mont-Dieu.*

16. The soul, which is more often free for from bodily desires, can have room in the hall of the mind; when the whole din of earthly concerns is silent, it may rejoice in holy meditations and in eternal delights. St. Leo in Sermon 8 on the fast of the 10th month and on almsgiving.

thy former, thou art far more sure to[17] fall more seldom, rise sooner, stand more securely, live more sweetly, and die more confidently. Go to, I say, why standest thou still? Why camest thou hither? Consider thy coarse habit, and see what penance it exacteth? Look upon the place and reflect what spirit it teacheth thee? Be courageous and make no delay, thy death is certain, and thy hour uncertain; the judge is at hand.[18] Alas! The pleasure of this world is short, but the punishment for it perpetual. A little suffering here and infinite glory hereafter.

Thus, this new soldier of Christ spent his time in holy discourses, sometimes of the majesty of Almighty God, sometimes of his own misery. Although his precedent conversation to religion was a mirror of perfection, yet he stood not still in that grace he had already gotten, but continually aspired to higher, in which he far excelled his fellow novices. Two virtues were chiefly eminent in him: simplicity and purity. He likewise had a perfect oblivion of all worldly things. He greedily desired and willingly accepted of the inferior and basest employments of the monastery. Neither did he esteem it a dishonor to him to cast himself at the feet of the friars, but was most willing to serve everyone at their beck. In this his first year, he laid such grounds of humility that in his whole life after he was a rare example and pattern of this virtue. Neither when he was promoted to superiority did he leave off his humble exercises. Thus going from grace to grace, from virtue to virtue, his good example was a burning lamp to give others light, to imitate his virtues, that the whole monastery began every day more and more to flourish in regular observance, and in the opinion of the world, to get a great name of sanctity.

---

17. In religion a person lives more purely, falls less often, gets up more quickly, advances more cautiously, rests more securely, is more frequently consoled. He is purged more quickly, dies more confidently, he is rewarded more abundantly. St. Bernard likewise, in the Homily [on the text] "The kingdom of heaven is like a businessman."

18. St. Francis's words, *Exhortation to the Brothers.*

Of His Natural Gifts, and of His Prudence and Mortification of His Eyes

He was an elected vessel, beautified with all the jewels of virtues, and as his mind was replenished with supernatural gifts, so his body wanted not its natural graces. He was of a spare body but comely, he had a grave and modest look, his eyes were sparkling tokens of the fire of divine love, which was in his soul invisible to the eye. There was not one member in that man which was not subordinate to the rule of reason. His speech was meek and humble, his conversation angelical. He had an excellent natural wit, joined with a happy memory. He had likewise a singular good judgment (as appeared in his government); he was courageous in going through with business, which did tend to the honor of Almighty God, and the good of religion; he was grateful to all, giving to everyone their due respect. He was dexterous in his actions, modest in correcting, and a peacemaker, reconciling those who upon any occasion had been at jars. In his sermons he was hot, but moving. In hearing of confessions he was a helper, a counsellor, and a comforter. In his ordinary speech he was not fawning, nor biting, and his conversation without any pertinacity. And to conclude all in a few words: he was a man of another world, of whom we may justly say as[19] Alexander Halensis said of St. Bonaventure, that he was a man in whom Adam seemed not to have sinned. He was a reformer, prelate, master, and pattern of perfection, of the Seraphical Order of our Holy Father St. Francis, who through so many provinces and remote kingdoms, illustrated this sacred institution; as another Apostle preordained by Almighty God for this happy end.

Of His Religious Simplicity, and Mortificatin of His Eyes

But to descend to particulars, wherein his religious simplicity was manifested. He was so absorbed in Almighty God that he minded nothing of exterior things. When he was a brother, keeping the keys of the

19. Antonio Possevino, S.J., in his "Apparatus Sacer" *Critical Apparatus on Ecclesiastical Writers*, vol. 1, from St. Bonaventure.

pantry, for the space of six months there were in the pantry grapes and pomegranates, which lay so palpably that none could choose but see them, but he, for that space, neither saw nor smelt, much less touched them. Being asked why he did not give them unto the brothers, he humbly answered that he knew of none that were there. Another time, living four years in another cloister, he never took notice of a great tree which stood in the midst of the court, which was obvious to everyone's eye. Being a year in another place and asked what his cell was made of, he answered, he knew not whether it was of stone, or brick, or wood. And a chapel which he frequented above others, yet he knew neither situation, form, or any ornament which did belong thereunto.

He was wont to say to blessed Teresa, his ghostly child, that he never knew a brother in his monastery, but only by his speech. Moreover, he was so mortified in his eyes that wheresoever he was, he knew no difference in places, no distance of cells. And, finally, he was a dead man to all exterior things. Neither was this mortification any stupidity of nature, or want of senses, but his continual busying his thoughts upon Almighty God, a more noble, and higher object. Who could but think this chaste child of St. Francis to have made a covenant with his eyes, not to behold a virgin? And well he might be styled that son of a dove, whose eyes were washed with the milk of innocence. He kept such a continual guard over his eyes that he never knew any woman by her face. There was a certain noble matron famous for her virtue, who was wont, at Placentia, sometimes to visit the holy Father for his spiritual counsel; she meeting him at Avila, saluted him, and expressed to him the difficulties of her state; he modestly denied that he ever saw the woman. If ever he opened his eyes, it was in the choir; though he had so good a memory that he knew most part of the office without book. Being Superior, he did particularly correct this imperfection with severity, knowing nothing to be more prejudicial to the soul than to set open those windows, at which doth enter the greater part of sin that doth defile the heart of man.

With What Austerity and Mortification the Holy Father Lived

Because for the most part this Holy Father lived in solitary convents, most remote from worldly tumults, or rather hermitages, all his rigorous penance could not be taken notice of by any. Nevertheless, we will set down some, which he could not hide from those with whom he conversed. He did wear, for seven years together, a hair shirt, full of hard knots. St. Teresa affirmeth that he wore it twenty years. Besides plates of iron, and other things wherewith he tyrannized ever his tender flesh. His disciplines were so frequent and bloody that he seemed rather the trunk of a tree than a human body. He would never cover his head although it rained ever so fast, or the sun shined ever so hot. His diet was so slender and mean, that, in his youth and old age he did eat nothing but brown bread, and the most musty crusts that he could find. If sometimes he recreated himself with a few boiled herbs, he would not be so delicious as to eat them with oil. Being Superior he caused as many beans and peas to be boiled at once as should serve the convent for seven days together, which austerity his subjects most willingly embraced, being glad, in some measure, to imitate their chief. But he seasoned his own portion with ashes, or some ungrateful liquor, lest his palate should take pleasure in his meat.

Mother Teresa hath heard his companions say that sometimes he lived eight days together without any meat or drink, especially when with more violence, he addicted himself to devotion. For he suffered in his prayers frequent raptures and ecstasies, of which (saith she) I am witness. He never drank wine, but water, though, for the infirmity of his stomach, it was prescribed to him by the physician. But he constantly refused it, saying that nothing was so repugnant to holy purity and abstinence as flesh and wine, the one being an enemy to chastity, the other to contemplation, both which, as long as he lived, by God's grace, he would enjoy. I will set down for the satisfaction of the devout reader the words of ever blessed Teresa, the glory and foundress of the discalced

Carmelites, to whom he was sometimes ghostly father, of whom she confesseth to have received much spiritual comfort; whose authority, by reason of her renowned sanctity, and living at the same time with him, is without control. Her words be these:

> Almighty God bereaved us of a man of admirable example, when he took out of this life Father Peter of Alcantara. The world, it seemeth, could endure no longer so great a perfection. They say, that our health is not so good; that now those times be past, this holy man was of this time, he was fat in spirit, as those of other ages; he had also the world under his feet, for, though we do not go barefoot, nor do such austere penance as he did, there are many things (as I have said elsewhere) to tread down the world withal. And our Lord teacheth them, when he seeth such a mind, as he gave, in great measure, to this holy man, which I speak of, to continue forty-seven years together in such austere penance, as all know. I will declare some part of it, for I know that it is all true. He told it to me and to another, from whom he concealed little, and the cause why he told it me was the great love which he bore me, and which our Lord gave him to defend me and encourage me in the time of so great necessity as that was, which I have spoken of, and will declare further. It seemeth to me, that he told me that he had slept no more than an hour and a half betwixt day and night for the space of forty years, and this was the greatest difficulty he found in his penance at the beginning, to overcome his sleep, and for this cause he did always either kneel or stand, and when he slept it was sitting, leaning his head against a little piece of wood, which he had driven into the wall. He could not lie down, though he would, for his cell, as is known, was no longer than four feet and a half. In all these years he never put on his capuche, how great sunshine or rain soever was; neither had he anything on his feet, nor other garment but his habit of coarse cloth, without any other thing next his skin, and this as straight as could be endured, and a short cloak of the same upon it. He told me that when it was very cold he did put it off, and opened the door and little window

of his cell; that afterwards, when he did put his cloak on again and shut his door, he might give some contentment and recreate his body, which before was frozen with cold. He did very ordinarily eat but once in three days, and he asked me at what I marvelled, for it was very possible for one that accustomed himself to it. His poverty was extreme, and likewise his mortification in his youth. With all his sanctity, he was very affable, though he used not many words, if he were not spoken to, for then he was very pleasing, having a good understanding.

And a little after,

His end was like his life, preaching and admonishing his friars. When he saw death draw nigh, he said the psalm: "I rejoiced in these things which were said to me" and kneeling down, departed. Since our Lord hath let me enjoy him more than in his life, giving me advice and counsel in many things, I have seen him many times in exceeding great glory. The first time he appeared unto me, he said, "O happy penance which did merit such a reward!" and many other things. A year before he died, he appeared to me, being absent, and I knew that he should die, and I sent him word, being some leagues from hence. When he gave up the ghost, he appeared to me and said that he went to rest; I believed it not. I told some of it, and eight days after the news came that he was dead, or rather began to live for ever. Behold here his austerity endeth with so great glory, he seemed to comfort me more than when he was in this world. Our Lord told me once, that nothing should be asked in his name which he would not hear. I have seen many things fulfilled, which I have desired him to ask of our Lord; he be blessed for ever. Amen.

And in the thirtieth chapter of her life, she sayeth as follows:

Our Lord vouchsafed to remedy a great part of my trouble, and for that time the whole, by bringing to this place the Blessed Father Peter of Alcantara, of whom I have already made mention, and spoken something of his penance; for amongst other things, I was certified, that for twenty years he had worn a cilice of plate continually. He is the author of certain little books of prayer, which are now much used in the Spanish tongue, for as one that hath exercised it well, he wrote very profitably, giving most excellent rules to those who addicted themselves to prayer. He observed the first rule of St. Francis with all rigor, and other things which I have related before.[20]

Thus she, and so much shall suffice to speak of, but part of his rigorous penance, it was his fervent zeal, and love of God, not strength of body, which made this crabbed way of penance easy to his heroic spirit; whose example may (though not in so great a measure as he did), justly move us to shake off that old and self-love excuse of ours, in saying our bodies are weak, when alas! our wills are frozen, and so nice, that we are afraid to expose our body but to a poor trial. The heathen Seneca will check our indevotion, who saith, "Not because certain things are hard, therefore we dare not do them, but because we dare not do them, therefore they are hard."

Of His Great Purity and Humility

The man of God increasing in his rigorous penance, did not only mortify in part, but wholly subdued his passions, and made his senses subordinate to the rule of reason; he suffered nothing to enter into his soul which might separate, or in the least kind withdraw his affection from his beloved spouse, for (as much as was possible for pilgrim man), he enjoyed the spirit of God; golden peace and divine consolation sat upon his wings of contemplation, and where others make their bodies masters, he made his a slave unto his spirit. Hence it came to pass that many of both sex, drawn with the fragrant odour of his virtues, flocked to him as to another Apostle, to whose counsels and admonitions they obeyed, as to a divine oracle.

---

20. From *The Life of St. Teresa of Avila*, ch. 27.

Upon a time, the Count Orapsane, a devout nobleman, came to visit him, and falling into discourse, how much Almighty God was moved with the sins of the world, out of his zeal breaketh into these speeches, O Father! what do you think? What will become of this wicked world? Do you think the divine justice can contain itself any longer from revenge? Behold, how virtue is oppressed, and sin triumpheth? How wilfully do we hoard up anger against the day of anger? To which the man of God modestly answered and said, noble Sir do not afflict yourself, a remedy will easily be found to cure this disease; the point of the difficulty consisteth only in you and me, for the general perdition of mankind floweth from this fountain, that all and everyone dissembling or cloaking their own sins accuse the whole, when the whole cannot be said to sin at all, but particular persons in the whole. Wherefore, men cry out against the wickedness of the world, that all are naught, and none that do good, when if they would but look into their own particular, they should find matter enough of sorrow, and to move themselves to do penance for their own faults; but now because they blame the whole, they neglect their own particulars, and justify themselves with a sottish presumption. Therefore, noble Sir, let your Lordship, and I, mend one a piece, and then a great part of the world will be amended; we shall appease the angry judge and repair a great part of the ruin of mankind by our good example.

When Charles the V recollected himself in a certain monastery of the Hieronymites, understanding of the sanctity and integrity of this holy Father, he sent for him, with an intent to make him his ghostly father. But he humbly refusing so great an honor, alleged some reasons why he thought this employment not to be fitting for him. At which denial, the Emperor being a little moved with anger, said, we charge you, Father, that you would take care of our soul. He seeing this sudden alteration of Cæsar, fell down at the feet of his majesty and earnestly desired him to defer the business to what day or hour he would please to appoint, that, in the meantime, he might commend it to Almighty

God, which the Emperor granted; then he took his leave of the Emperor and said, this, renowned Cæsar, shall be a sign unto you, that it is not according to the will of God, which you have desired, if I do not return at the appointed time. Then passing to his former solitude, as he went, he complained with many sighs and groans to Almighty God, fearing by the devices of Satan, to be drawn from the embracings of his blessed spouse, Jesus Christ. He sent up his fervent prayers to the Almighty's throne, and said these or like words:

> Lord, I have not, therefore, left the world, and betaken myself to this holy desert, that now at length my name should be renowned in a prince's court, and live in honor, that am a poor Franciscan friar. Why should my ears be troubled with flatterings of courtiers, who came to speak my fault in religion? I confess that this office may be exercised without sin; but whether it be expedient for my soul, sweet Jesus, tell me? And when he entered into his cell, Lord, I beseech thee, pull me not from hence, whither thy omnipotent hand hath brought me. Here I am safe, here I am rich; because I enjoy thee, who alone can satiate my soul. Alas! without thee what is the whole empire? And with thee, this poor cell is a kingdom of content. Here, let me live. Here, let me die. Lord, let it please thee what I wish for, because all is thine whatsoever I desire. If thou grantest me thy petition, let this be a sign unto me, that Caesar molesteth me no more.

So rising, as being heard, did appear no more before him. Neither did the Emperor ever solicit him after.

The same request did the illustrious Princess Joanna, sister to Philip II, Catholic King of Spain, make unto this holy Father, whom he likewise denied after the same manner. Thus, whilst he fled honors, he was most honored of all, and reverenced of everyone. And what candid sincerity he used in contemning proffered honors, men of no small quality observed, that those who honored him, he would no more regard their speech than a simple idiot, and would labor to divert them from that to some other discourse. He had rather be called a sinner than a holy man, and he himself would (without scandal) lay open to the world his imperfections, under which, his virtues and graces were cloaked. But God, the searcher of secrets, by how much he did strive to hide them; the more he made his fame to shine in the world, to the astonishment of all. For he was a man whom God had chosen according to his own heart, by whose industry, and from whose spiritual loins did spring many servants of Jesus Christ and many renowned martyrs of our holy order.

Of His Fervent Prayers and Raptures, and of His Spirit of Prophecy

Almighty God was always present with him, and he with God. His soul was like a fiery furnace, made hot with the fuel of the Cross of Christ. It was not in his own power to contain himself, but what thing soever he either saw, or heard, which might delight his beloved Jesus, though it were but afar off, his heartstrings would begin to tremble, and his vital spirits leave him, and frequently fall into ecstasy. He was accustomed for a whole hour together to say his prayers with his arms stretched out in the manner of a cross, sighing and weeping, till at last he would be beside himself, elevated from the ground, and united only to his God. He was oftentimes in this manner rapt when he was in the choir at matins. But his devotion was much more augmented at the altar, when he celebrated the dreadful sacrifice: then would rivers of tears gush in abundance from his venerable eyes, that would move the most stony and obdurate heart of any of the standers by unto compunction. After Mass he would withdraw himself into his cell, where he hath been often heard to have had grievous conflicts with devils, who oftentimes appearing in a visible shape, would follow him up and down with terrible fury.

In talking of Almighty God his soul would be presently inebriated with divine sweetness, and ascending by degrees from one word to another, as, "What! Was God incarnated for me? Was God made man for me? Was God vested with human flesh for me?" and the like. He would forthwith break into exclamations, and hurrying himself into his cell, would for the space of above three hours together, lose the use of his senses.[21] One day, a brother that was newly made Priest, practising in the garden to sing Mass, when he heard him sing these words of St. John's Gospel, "And the Word was made flesh" he became enraptured and remained for a long time in ecstasy.

This, therefore, was ordinary to the friend of God, that when he heard anything of the humanity of our blessed Savior, or any devout word of the Holy Scripture, it would cause him raptures. Neither could he help them, though he did strive much against them, especially in the presence of others, but his heart would become like melting wax in the midst of his bowels. He was often, in seeing the crucifix, moved with such compassion that his arms would be rapt across, with little clouds glittering about his head. He would sometimes prophesy, to some the loss of honors, to others sudden death, to others purgatory; which would fall out the very day and hour he told them. The first time he saw St. Teresa, he told her what contradictions and afflictions she suffered from her ghostly fathers and other spiritual persons, who would needs persuade her, that she was seduced; and, moreover, that she was to suffer much more in the same kind. He likewise foretold what should be the success in the Indies.

Of His Patience

He traced the steps of our blessed Savior, and all his glorious saints,[22] all which did never merit their crowns without carrying of the Cross of Christ. He was another patient Job, in suffering the temptations and afflictions the infirmity of man is subject unto; he was in a particular manner loaded with the heavy burden of them, notwithstanding his fervent spirit, patiently supported, and victoriously triumphed over all

---

21. Marianus, *Life of St. Peter of Alcantara*, ch. 10.
22. "Which of the saints has been crowned without suffering? Solomon was only among pleasures, and perhaps that was the reason he fell." St. Jerome.

his difficulties, even over all the force of Satan. His frequent combats, his persecutions, his sickness, his long and tedious travels, the difficulties he did undergo in erecting his province, would take up too much time to relate. He was so greedy of suffering that he esteemed himself happy to bear afflictions for the name of Jesus, saying that there was no way so sure and easy to attain unto perfection as the carrying of the Cross of Christ.

He would, therefore, beg of Almighty God, that he might never be without some affliction. Thus did our courageous champion trample upon his enemies. Thou shall walk upon the Asp and the Basilisk; and thou shall trample underfoot the Lion and the Dragon (Ps 90). Whilst he vanquished all his foes, not so much by resisting, as by suffering.

Of His Charity Towards His Neighbor

His charity towards his neighbour was unspeakable; for this cause he often visited hospitals to serve the sick, assisting them both spiritually and corporally, and oftentimes miraculously restoring them to their former health. After he had made an end of his devotion, the residue of his time he spent in comforting the afflicted, in cherishing the feeble, and, finally, in anything he could imagine might comfort his neighbour, either corporally or spiritually; so that innumerable people of all conditions and sexes continually flocked unto him for his charitable assistance.

Of His Poverty

He was a rigid observer of holy poverty, which in imitation of his patron,[23] St. Francis, he not only loved, but honored so far that he was wont to call it the Evangelical pearl, wherewith he enriched his new province, in that lustre as the observance was in the infancy of our

---

23. St. Francis was not only enjoying the goods of poverty most willingly, but also he was thus glorifying it and cultivating it, that should I have sought for the smallest part of poverty, indeed no human dignity would be able to be compared. Therefore as St. Bonaventure writes, in every sermon he was calling [poverty] at one time "Mother," at another "Spouse," sometimes "Lady" but often even "Queen," because she shone forth so outstandingly in the the King of kings and his mother. Jerome Platus, *On the Happiness of the Religious State*, Bk. 2, ch. 3.

Seraphical Order, from which time, and by whose example, most provinces through the Christian world have excelled in this particular point, as much as in their former splendour. He permitted his brethren to have nothing in their cells except of mere necessity, and to the preachers he permitted them no more than two or three books, with the Bible and a crucifix.

He was upon a time asked by St. Teresa, whether or not she should found her monasteries with rents and yearly revenues, to which diverse persons of quality had advised her. He answered that it was an injury to God the author of Evangelical counsels to ask the advice of men touching the observance of them, or to doubt whether or not they were observable. And with all encouraged her to be constant in that fervent desire she had begun in embracing holy poverty. To whose counsel she willingly obeyed. And after, our Lord appeared to her in prayer, and declared, that it was his will that her monasteries should be founded in holy poverty. His letter to her, I think it not amiss, to set down at large, which followeth.

A Letter of the Blessed Father Fr. Peter De Alcantara, to the Holy Mother Teresa of Jesus, Who Demanded His Counsel, Whether She Should Found Monasteries With Rents or Not

The Holy Ghost give you his grace and love, etc. I received yours, delivered me by Don Gonzales d'Aranda, and am amazed considering your zeal and piety. In committing to the direction of learned lawyers, that which is noways their profession, or belonging unto them, you should do well to take their advice concerning the deciding of a process, or of suits in law, and temporal affairs, but in that which concerns perfection of life, we ought to treat only with those who practise the same. For such as the conscience of everyone is, such are his exercises and works. Concerning the Evangelical counsels, may I demand whether they be observable or not? For that the counsels of God cannot be but good, neither can the observance thereof seem difficult, unless to those who govern themselves according to human prudence, having less confidence in God than they ought. For he who hath given the counsel will consequently give force and means to accomplish the same. And if your zeal and fervour draw you to embrace the counsels of Jesus Christ, observe them with the greatest integrity and perfection that you possibly can, seeing they were equally given to both sexes. It cannot be, but the same merit and reward will be rendered unto you, as to others that have truly observed them. And if there be seen any want or necessity in the monasteries of poor religious women, it is because they are poor against their wills, and not through fault of their vow of poverty, or following of Evangelical counsels. For I account not much of their simple poverty, but of their patient sufferance of the same for the love of God. But I more esteem that poverty which is desired, procured, and embraced for the same love.

And, if I should think, or determinately believe otherwise, I should not hold myself a good Catholic. I believe in this, and in all other things taught by our blessed Savior, and that his counsels are good and profitable, as proceeding from God, and though they oblige not to sin, they bind, nevertheless, that man to be more perfect that followeth them, than if he had not undertaken them at all. I hold them poor in spirit, who are poor in will, as our Savior hath said, and myself proved; however, I believe more from God than of my own experience, that those, who by the grace of God are with all their hearts poor, lead a life most happy, as confiding and hoping in him alone. His divine Majesty give you light to understand this truth and to practise it. Believe not those that shall tell you the contrary, for want of light and understanding, or for not having tasted how sweet our Lord is to those that fear and love him, renouncing for his sake all unnecessary things of this world, for they are enemies of the Cross of Christ, not believing the glory which accompanieth the same. I also pray our Lord to give you this light, that you be not wanting in the belief of this truth, so much manifested; and that you take not counsel but of the followers of Jesus Christ; although others think it sufficient, if they observe the thing they are bound unto, yet they have not always greater virtue and perfection by their work. And though the counsel be good, yet that of our blessed Savior is much better, who knows what he *counsels, and gives grace to accomplish the same, and in the end reward to those who hope in him, and not in rents and goods of the earth.*

From Avila, this 14th day of April, 1562

Of His Confidence in Almighty God's Providence

His admirable confidence in the providence of Almighty God accompanied his rigid and Evangelical poverty, and it oftentimes miraculously appeared both at home and abroad. He[24] lived sometimes in the convent of Sancta Maria de Rosario, which is situated in a woody place, by the river Tentairis, six Italian miles remote from any company; at all times it was difficult to come to it, as the way was very steep and crooked,[25] nevertheless it was a place of great devotion, whither the inhabitants of the country much resorted; but now, by reason of a great snow, the like of which was not seen in the memory of man, the monastery was so environed on every side, that the friars could not go out to get their victuals, neither could any come to them to bring provision. They cried to heaven to the Father of the poor, that being destitute of all human aid, he only, out of his infinite mercy, would be pleased not to forsake them.

The Holy Father desired them to go into the church, and kneeling down before the Blessed Sacrament, to pray to God that he would put a remedy to their hard affliction. He with great confidence animated his brethren, saying "Be courageous, brethren. Almighty God will not be long, he will come without delay." He had no sooner uttered the words, but another most violent storm of snow fell so fast, that frustrated the hopes of all human assistance. But he that containeth not his anger long did not delay to comfort his afflicted children. Behold! a little space after the storm was over, the porter heard the bell of the gate of the convent ring; he went to open the door, but espied nobody; he returned back

---

24. Marianus, *Life of St. Peter of Alcantara*, ch. 6.
25. The difficulty of the journey to him was such that on account of the solitude of the place and the crookedness of the roads, it was scarcely even open for neighbors and people accustomed to it. Gonzaga: Part 3 of the *Chronicles of the Order of St. Francis in the Province of Saint Joseph.*

again, thinking it to be the wind that had stirred the bell, or that his fancy seemed to hear the noise when he heard it not; checking himself with foolishness, that he could imagine that it was possible for anyone to come to the convent in so deep a snow. Whilst he was thus discoursing with himself, it rang again so hard that all heard it, notwithstanding there was a great wind.

Then returning again to the gate, and opening it, he found a basket filled with new white bread, he looked about to see if he could espy anybody, but no creature appeared, for it was a deep snow, where the footing of any person could not but appear. He left the basket, and with joy ran back into the convent to carry the good news to the friars, who would not believe, until the holy Father commanded all the brothers to go in manner of procession to see what Almighty God had done for his servants; when they came, they found all true, as the porter had related to them; but their benefactor did nowhere visibly appear. They carried the basket in, and after thanksgiving, refreshed themselves with the bread which the Father of heaven had miraculously bestowed upon them. Upon which they lived many days, until the extremity of the season was past, and they could go out to beg alms according to their custom.

Another time[26] travelling in the extremity of the heat of summer upon the mountain vulgarly called Sierra Morena, he, with his companion grew so faint, for want of something to quench their thirst, that they were ready to sink under the burden of their tedious journey. He said unto his companion, Brother, let us betake ourselves to prayer, the only remedy to incline the God of mercy to take compassion upon our misery. Whilst they were upon their knees at prayers, from a thicket came running out a mad bull, which made towards them amain; they seeing themselves in this great danger of their lives, betook themselves to flight, but the bull pursued them over hedge and ditch, hard at their heels, till at last he forced them to a place where there was a fountain of water; when they came in sight of that, the bull, forgetting his former

---

26. Marianus, *Life of St. Peter of Alcantara*, ch. 7.

fury, stood still like an innocent lamb; he breathed himself awhile, and went another way. But they admiring this great miracle of the Omnipotent, that sendeth his wild beasts to teach the poor, refreshed themselves, and went on their journey with alacrity, their souls more comforted with this unexpected benefit of Almighty God's providence, than their bodies strengthened with the water which they drank for their sustenance.

Having occasion[27] to go from De las Lucuas to Del Pico, as he was on his journey it began to snow, which fell so fast that it was not possible for him to go forward or backward, so that he was enforced to remain the whole night in that extremity of cold and snow. But the fervour of his devotion, wherewith he implored the divine assistance, caused him to pass over the night without tediousness. But what was more admirable, behold! in the morning when it was day, one might see that the snow did not so much as touch or wet him, but it congealed over his head, in a miraculous manner, like a canopy, and on each side two walls of snow frozen in a curious manner defended him from the inclemency of the weather, as though he had been shut in a beautiful chamber.

These few miracles I have set down, collected out of many, which Almighty God hath been pleased to work by the means of his glorious servant, as testimonies,[28] not only of many singular prerogatives of graces exhibited to this holy Father in his own particular; but also, that we, admiring the strange and unaccustomed manner of Almighty God's proceedings with this blessed man, the truth whereof being confirmed by many approved authors, may be incited to imitate his virtues, whom God hath honored with the grace of working miracles. If thou shouldst object with Calvin, In Præfat. Instit., that the miracles of our saints in the Catholic Church are partly feigned, partly diabolical, I answer, that the same thing the Pharisees objected to our blessed Savior, that he cast out devils in Beelzebub the prince of the devils. Moreover, it is most

---

27. Ibid.
28. I call a "miracle" whatever difficult or unusual thing appears above hope or the ability of the wonderer. Certain [miracles] produce wonder, certain [miracles] produce great grace and goodwill. St. Augustine, *On the Usefulness of Belief*, ch 16.

devilish to blemish the integrity of the ancient fathers and saints, with such an impudent and foul aspersion, as those who wrote the lives of other saints, as Nyssens of Thaumaturgus, St. Athanasius and St. Jerome of St. Anthony, Severus of St. Martin, St. Gregory of St. Benedict, St. Bernard of St. Malachias, St. Bonaventure of St. Francis, whose authority if we should deny, no faith or credit is to be given to any history in the world, which absurdity none but men out of their wits, or blinded with malice, will admit. St. Augustine confirmeth what I say. His words are these: "For will someone say that these miracles are false, and they had not been done, but had been written falsely? Whoever says this, if he denies that these letters ought to be believed, he must also say that neither do any of the gods take care of mortal affairs."[29]

Of His Knowledge in Holy Scripture, and of His Preaching

He was so well versed in the Holy Scripture, that for the most part, he could repeat it without book, and in explicating it, he was so clear, and withal so moving, that one might judge his learning to be rather supernaturally infused in prayer than naturally gotten by the ordinary means of study,[30] for he quickly learned what he was taught, seeing he had the Holy Ghost for his master. He wrote some spiritual works, wherein he had a special gift from Almighty God, both to direct those who tend to perfection in their journey towards heaven, as also to inflame their wills to aspire to that eternal good. In this particular science he was chiefly eminent, and wrote profitable and learned tracts of this matter. He had such a rare gift in preaching, such invective against sin, and withal so comfortable to those who were pulling their feet out of the snare of vices, that Almighty God was pleased to work by his means many wonderful effects in the souls of his auditory.

In the city of Abula, Avila there was a young gentleman who was given up to and, as it were, buried in all the sports and vanities of this

---

29. *The City of God*, Bk. 10, ch. 18.
30. "O how swiftly working is the word of wisdom, and where God is the teacher, how quickly is learned what is taught." Bl. Leo, Sermon 1 on Pentecost.

wicked world, but especially in the wild and pernicious love of wanton women. Coming in his pomp upon a festival day of that place, he by chance met the holy father; and, when he understood from his companions the quality and sanctity of him, he went towards him, with others, to salute him with great respect, and withal begged his prayers, but God knoweth with what intention, for he still obstinately remained in his filthy desires. But the holy father in his sermon touched the core of his soul unto the quick, (yet not revealing any person) insomuch that the Holy Ghost did so work with him, that this prodigal child understanding the father was to go away from that place the next day, made haste to get pen and ink to write his sins, the next day cometh to the father and saluteth him, giving him a long[31] scroll of his sinful life, and desired him for the love of God, that he would vouchsafe to pray for him, that God would have mercy upon his soul, and that he would not punish him for ever according to his deserts. The holy father received his paper and promised that he would pray for him.

So each departed their way. But he had scarce turned his back, but the father earnestly begged of Almighty God his conversion, of which he was presently sensible; for, before he came home, the spirit of God did so inflame him, that he abjured his former conversation, and loathed the pleasures that before he loved so much, and being returned to his house, flung off his brave clothes, tore his chain from his neck, and vested himself in mean and country clothes, without any shame of appearing to all the world, all admiring the sudden change of the right hand of the Most High; and, as afterwards, he lived well, persevering to the end, so he died happily. He dispersed his patrimony amongst the poor, and built many monasteries and hospitals, as testimonies of his conversion.

He had such efficacy in his preaching, that many common women, drawn with the sweetness of his spirit, changed their sordid and base habits of living into holy and pious conversation. Others, as well

---

31. The young man, out of humility, manifested his sins to the holy father out of the Sacrament of Confession.

of the nobility as amongst the meaner sort of people, renouncing all pleasures for the love of Jesus, shrouded themselves in cloisters, where they might be secure from the contagion of worldly vanities. And many consecrating their virginity to their celestial spouse, like lilies amongst thorns, persevered in the open world amidst the dangers thereof, with immoveable constancy.

Of His Religious Zeal and of His Death

The reverend esteem of his virtue increased so much, even in his own cloister, that there, many times (enjoined by obedience) performing the office of Guardian with great integrity, he was, at length, by the suffrages of all the fathers, elected twice Provincial of the province of St. Gabriel, where he made a happy and notable reformation. But after his three years expired, he betook himself again to his poor hermitage, where he feasted his soul with sacred contemplation, persevering in reading the ancient fathers, watchings, fastings, and regular discipline. But the more he hid himself in these obscure places, the more the fame of his learning and sanctity did shine abroad. And in testimony that Almighty God would not have this resplendent light to be put under a bushel, but to be set upon a candlestick, to give light to others to follow his glorious footsteps, and to the end that he might not only enrich his own soul with the treasures of virtue, but also instruct others, both by his doctrine and example, to aspire to heaven, the apostolic see did vouchsafe to honor him with a commission, by virtue of which, he should erect and found a new province, under the title of St. Joseph; which, before his death, he was so happy to see, not only multiplied in number of convents and religious men, by his great labor and travail, but also to be perfectly established in regular observance and true monastical discipline.

At last, the number of his merits being complete, his just master, whom he had served so long with great fidelity, was pleased to call him to reward his labors with an eternal crown of glory, and to reap in joy what he had sown in tears. He fell sick in the convent of St. Andrew de Monte Areno, where Almighty God vouchsafed to let him know the hour of his death. And before his departure he called his brethren, exhorting them to perseverance in that happy course which they had undertaken for the love of God and the saving of their own souls. He then received upon his knees, with abundance of tears, the sacred Viaticum with singular devotion, and a little after, his infirmity increasing, he received also the Sacrament of Extreme Unction. The Blessed Virgin and St. John, to whom all his life he was very much devout, appeared to him and gave him assurance of his salvation; which ever-comfortable news he no sooner understood, but his heart was ravished with joy, and his mouth filled with gladness, and out of that abundance of content he breaketh out into these words of the prophet David, "I have rejoiced in those things that are said unto me: we will go into the house of our Lord" (Ps 112). In fine, the happy hour being come, he yielded his blessed soul into the hands of his maker, and by the passage of a temporal death, travelled to an eternal life, on the 18th of October, upon the feast of St. Luke, 1562, the 63rd year of his age, and the 47th of his entrance into holy religion. His body after his death became more beautiful, shining with great clarity, and sending forth sweet odours. The people from all parts flocked to behold this sacred spectacle, and greedy after so rich a prey, clipped pieces of his habit, which they conserved as holy relics. His body was no sooner in the grave, but his sepulchre began to be renowned with many miracles[32] of which for brevity's sake I omit to speak of, because I would not be too tedious to the devout reader.

His soul was no sooner out of his body,[33] but presently he appeared to St. Teresa, to bring unto her the joyful tidings of his reception into heaven. Many times after he appeared to her, and once, amongst the rest, he said unto her, "O happy penance that deserved such a glorious

---

32. When an Ethiopian boy was lead to his tomb by his mistress, wife of a certain Martin of Friars and neighbour of the aforementioned town of Arrenae, he was restored to health by his merits, the best and greatest God working through him. And Leonora Gonsalva, inhabitant of the same town who was suffering most terribly from paralysis was also freed at his tomb. Francis Gonzaga, of the *Chronicles of the Seraphic Order*, part 3. See more in John of St. Mary in his life of the Blessed [Peter of] Alcantara, ch. 30.

33. Marianus, *Life of St. Peter of Alcantara*, ch. 27.

recompense."[34] Happy, indeed,[35] was his penance that changed sorrows into pleasures, mourning into mirth, tears into joys, and a momentary cross into an eternal crown. The same blessed Teresa, as we have said before, affirmed that she received more comfort and consolation from him after his death than in the time of his life; and that his soul flew immediately to heaven, without any passage by purgatory. All these things being well examined and verified by persons, without all exception, worthy of credit, His Holiness, for the glory of God, honor of the saint, and benefit of the faithful, vouchsafed to pronounce him beatified, to the end that, as he had a perfect fruition of glory in the Church triumphant, so he should want no praise or reverence in the Church militant. He was beatified on the 18th of April, 1622, and his office is celebrated in the convents of his order on the 19th of October.

---

34. Our works do not have the meritorious goodness of glory from their own nature, nor from ours, but from God. For our works are to be taken in a twofold respect. 1. As they are in their proper nature and dignity; 2. As they have God's promise and acceptance. If we consider them in the first sense, so they do not merit salvation; if in the second they do. This I say to answer the objection of ignorant Protestants, who might take occasion to carp at this word (deserved), and who likewise think that we so dignify our works that thereby we think to merit heaven, abstracting from the merits of our blessed Savior's Passion, when it is certain our doctrine is that the chief reason of merit is founded in God's promise, not man's work; and our works so to merit and to be ennobled, chiefly by virtue of their principal agent our blessed Savior's Passion. Conrad Kling, *On the Common Passages*, vol. 1, part 1, ch. 35; Stapleton, *Controversies*, vol. 1, part 10, ch. 12; Bellarmine, *On Justification*, ch. 21 and vol. 1, part 5, ch. 11 with the Common of Doctors.

35. If the conversion of sinners, and of grievous sinners, be so pleasing to Almighty God that the angels of heaven do rejoice at it, according to St. Bernard, "Finally the fragrance of penance even reaches the heavenly mansions of the blessed so that, the Truth itself giving witness, there is great joy among the angels of God over one sinner doing penance. Rejoice, O penitents; be comforted, O weak of heart. I say this to you who recently were converted from the world, and who are withdrawing from your wicked ways, soon bitterness and confusion of the penitent soul rescued you, just as the pain of recent wounds is too aggravating. Let your hands, safe from trouble, distill the bitterness of myrrh into healing ointment; 'because God will not despise a contrite and humble heart'" (St. Bernard: *Sermon on the Song of Songs* 10). I say if such a conversion be so pleasing to God, how glorious may we judge this holy Father's penance to be, who from his cradle to his grave lived innocently and austerely? So that we may justly say of him as the Church of St. John, "You sought the desert caves while still in your tender years, fleeing the crowds of citizens, so that you might at least not be able to stain your life as a frivolous priest."

RESOURCES FOR CONTINUED EXPLORATION ON THE TOPIC OF PRAYER AND THE INTERIOR LIFE

- *Navigating the Interior Life* by Dan Burke, Emmaus Road Publishing
- *Fulfillment of All Desire* by Ralph Martin, Emmaus Road Publishing
- For articles, blog posts, and videos on the interior life: *SpiritualDirection.com*
- For formal education in spiritual theology: *Avila-Institute.com*

NAVIGATING THE INTERIOR LIFE

SPIRITUAL DIRECTION AND THE JOURNEY TO GOD

DANIEL BURKE
WITH FR. JOHN BARTUNEK, LC, STL

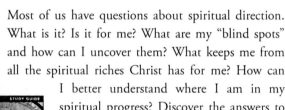

Most of us have questions about spiritual direction. What is it? Is it for me? What are my "blind spots" and how can I uncover them? What keeps me from all the spiritual riches Christ has for me? How can I better understand where I am in my spiritual progress? Discover the answers to these questions and more. Daniel Burke's *Navigating the Interior Life* will give you the tools you need to understand how and why we grow and die in the spiritual life and what we can do about it.

AVAILABLE in Spanish!

978-1-937155-86-5 // $13.95 // paperback
$39.95 // audiobook
$12.95 // audiobook download

Navigating the Interior Life Study Guide is designed to help you better understand the trajectory of your soul and to go deeper in your relationship with God. It leads you, step-by-step, through reflecting on essential material and answering personal questions that will help you discover God's will for your life through spiritual direction. Each chapter of this Study Guide includes a brief summary of material covered in *Navigating the Interior Life* and poses questions for reflection. A glossary of terms at the back helps you gain a better grasp on spiritual direction and become more literate in the faith. 978-1-940329-94-9 // $9.95 // paperback

emmausroad.org • (800) 398-5470

CPSIA information can be obtained at www.ICGtesting.com
Printed in the USA
BVOW07*1236280515

400904BV00005B/2/P